PEANUT BUTTER FOR CUPCAKES
A True Story From The Great Depression

Donna Nordmark Aviles

For Justin Ruby
Enjoy!
Donna N. Aviles

Wasteland Press

Shelbyville, KY USA
www.wastelandpress.net

Peanut Butter For Cupcakes:
A True Story From The Great Depression
by Donna Nordmark Aviles

Third Printing – September 2014
ISBN: 978-1-60047-076-9
Back cover photo: Oliver, Jr., Bud, May, Benny, Jim and
Margaret Nordmark

Printed in the U.S.A.

0   1   2   3   4

*Dedicated with love to Oliver & Estella's Children: May, Bud,
Oliver, Margaret, Jim and Ben Nordmark*

And

*In Memory of Wendell and Alice Wicks Who Turned Peanut
Butter Into Cupcakes!*

*Based on the Oral Histories of
Benjamin E. Nordmark, Sr.
James B. Nordmark
Oliver E. Nordmark*

*With contributing information and photographs from
Margaret L. Baabe, Laura May Greene, Ed Hall and Ted Hall*

Estella Rarick as a Young Girl

INTRODUCTION

The single word that could perhaps best describe the period of American history known as the Great Depression is perseverance. When the stock market collapsed on October 29, 1929, people from all walks of life were affected. Ordinary people, from doctors to waitresses, had invested their life savings in stocks and were suddenly penniless. Industry responded to the collapse by drastically cutting back production levels since no one had the ability to buy their goods. Workers were subsequently laid off from their jobs and thousands of businesses were soon forced to close.

In the face of record unemployment and bread lines that stretched for blocks, the spirit of the average American fought to stay strong and find innovative ways to survive until the country could recover and opportunities would again be available to every hardworking man.

Peanut Butter For Cupcakes is the tale of one family who lived through this historic time. Based on the memories of the Nordmark children, it is a testimony to the resilience and ingenuity of childhood. Although life served nothing more than peanut butter, each grew to find the sweetness of cupcakes as they reached for the American Dream through hard work and love of family.

CHAPTER ONE

The Indian Queen Hotel

May, 1930

"Please Oliver. It will only be until you can find work again," Estella pleaded to her husband of eleven years.

"I said no. I'm the man of the house and it's my job to provide for the family," was Oliver's obstinate reply. "My wife is not going to be seen working in the hotel Coffee Shoppe when I'm perfectly capable of putting in a full day's work."

"If there was a full day's work to be had," Estella mumbled under her breath. "Oliver, look," she pleaded into the eyes of her husband that held the pride of a man who had always been able to fend for himself. "Ever since the country fell into this depression there've been lots of men who can't find work. You've worked hard, but some things are just out of our control. We have six children that need to know where their next meal is coming from. I'm sure I can get the job at the Indian Queen Hotel and just as soon as you find work again, I'll be out of there the same day. Everyone's fallen on hard times, Oliver, and folks have to do whatever they can to get by. This is something I can do. Please let me go down and

1

The Indian Queen Hotel, Stroudsburg, PA

apply for that job."

Oliver walked slowly to the back of the house with his hands thrust deep into his empty pockets. He shuffled across the dirt floor of the back room kicking thoughtfully at the ground as he watched little clouds of dirt billow up. Ever since the stock market had crashed last October, things had gone from bad to worse. So many people had bought large amounts of stock with very little money down and it totally destabilized the whole system. Even though Oliver had not invested in the stock market, it didn't matter. As weeks and months wore on, everyone was affected with job layoffs and there was truly no end in sight. As he tried to decide what to do, three-and-a-half-year-old Jim came into the room and crouched in the corner watching his dad, so deep in thought. Estella cautiously joined them.

"What do you say?" she pleaded one last time to Oliver.

Oliver glanced at little Jim, then towards the front of the house where his youngest son Benny lay napping. He raised his head to meet Estella's eyes with a look of defeat.

"The minute I find work or get called back to the mill, you'll quit, right?"

"The very minute," was Estella's comforting reply.

"Well, you'd better get down there before someone else gets there before you," Oliver said as he forced a half smile at his pretty young wife.

"Oh thank you Oliver! You won't be sorry, I promise you. I'm sure I'll get the job and just as soon as you get work I'll be happy to quit," she bubbled with excitement. "I'll just grab my sweater and get right over to the hotel!" She hurried to the front room, grabbed her green cotton sweater and headed out the door.

* * * *

Estella paused only a moment as she reached for the handles of the heavy oak double doors of the Indian Queen Hotel, which was easily the largest and most elegant hotel on Main Street.

"I can do this," she said under her breath. "I need to get this job."

She heaved the doors open and passed into the lobby of the grand hotel. Keeping her eyes fixed forward and her head held high, she walked with purpose across the diamond-tiled flooring straight to the glass doors of the Coffee Shoppe. The sign on the door read **Help Wanted – Waitress 6:30am to 3:00pm. Start immediately.** Estella grabbed the sign off the door and entered the Coffee Shoppe.

"I'm here to apply for this waitress job," she said with conviction to the lady who stood near the hostess station.

"You'll need to speak with Mr. McGinn," she responded as she glanced up from the menu she was reading. "He's got another lady in there right now so you might as well come back later."

"If it's all the same to you, I'd like to wait to speak with him now," Estella said a bit desperately. "I need this job."

"Suit yourself," the hostess replied. "I'll let you know when he's available."

Estella felt a small sense of pride that she had not let the hostess push her back out the front door. She became even more determined to leave with the job. As she waited, Estella walked slowly around the Coffee Shoppe, gently touching the linen tablecloths and absently turning over the silver serving pieces. This would be a nice place to work, she thought to herself. She might even make a little extra money in tips if she was lucky. The people she knew would never be able to afford to eat in a place like this. Everyone she knew was struggling just to get by with the country in such a mess. If she could just get this job until Oliver was called back to the silk mill…

"Can I help you?" a tall gentleman in a sharp suit asked as his words broke into Estella's thoughts.

Quickly composing herself, Estella replied, "Yes, I'm here for the waitress job," as she handed the gentleman his **Help Wanted** sign.

"Yes, yes, isn't every woman in town coming in for that position," Mr. McGinn mused. "Come into my office then."

Estella followed Mr. McGinn into his lavishly furnished office as he motioned her to a fancy chair covered in beautiful tapestry. She quickly sat straight upright, with a slight forward lean. She didn't even give him time to speak.

"My name is Estella Nordmark, Mr. McGinn, and I know I'd be perfect for this job," she spoke quickly. "My husband has been out of work for some time and there are six children to be supported. If I can just get this job, we can manage until my husband finds new work or is called back to Zaleschitz's Silk Mill. I'll do a good job, I'm very reliable, and I can be here every morning at six o'clock. Anything I don't know how to do, I'll learn quickly. Please give me a chance, I really need this job," Estella pleaded as she finally took a breath.

"Well, you certainly are a determined woman," Mr. McGinn considered aloud as he stood and walk around the back of Estella's chair. "All the silk mills have shut down, what with the labor difficulties they've been having. You may be at this longer than you expect. Are you sure you're up for that?"

"I'll prove myself to be one of your best employees, Mr. McGinn," Estella replied firmly. "If you give me a chance, you won't be sorry."

"Do you have a resume with you?" Mr. McGinn asked, knowing full well she did not.

"Well, no, I don't have a resume. This will be my first paying job." Estella felt her hands start to shake from nervousness. "But I have lots of experience preparing and serving meals – I have

6

six children after all. And I'm very friendly, I get along with everyone, and most importantly I'm a fast learner."

"You don't have any waitress experience, Mrs. Nordmark," Mr. McGinn began. "But I like your determination. The job is yours if you can start tomorrow at six o'clock in the morning."

Estella all but jumped from her chair. She grabbed Mr. McGinn's hand, shaking it wildly. "Thank you, thank you, sir. You won't be disappointed, I promise you. I'll be here at six in the morning!" She grabbed her small purse and bounced out the door beaming with pride at her accomplishment!

* * * *

Estella May Nordmark arrived at the Indian Queen Hotel Coffee Shoppe promptly the next morning at 6:00 am. It was Friday, the 23rd of May and the smell of summer was in the air. She wasn't sure just how long she would need this job, but while it was hers, she intended to do her best and make her family proud of her. At the age of twenty-six, it was her first real job. Of course being a mother to six children between the ages of one and ten was a big job in itself, but no paycheck was issued for that important work and food had to be put on the table. This waitress job would hopefully be enough to hold the family over until the silk workers' union charter was approved and

7

labor negotiations could begin in earnest with the owners of the mills.

Estella knew that couldn't happen soon enough for Oliver. In the eleven years of their marriage, since she was fifteen, she had always known that he was a hard worker. He had worked in the glass factories of Corning, NY when they were first wed. When that job ended, he re-enlisted in the Navy and sent all of his pay back to her and their first child, May. When he was home on leave in 1921, Oliver knew he had to do better for his young family so he headed back to Kansas where he had grown up. He soon found work following the harvest and quickly sent for his wife and daughter. In 1922, their first son Francis Henry was born in Kansas. Estella had named him for her brother Henry and borrowed her father's middle name of Francis. Oliver took to calling his son 'Bud' from the very beginning. Estella thought back to their years in Kansas fondly. Oliver had taught her how to ride a horse, which she found very frightening at first, but soon came to enjoy. They never had much money but they always seemed to get by on Oliver's resourcefulness and charm. Eventually they found their way back East when Oliver got word of a tannery job in Stroudsburg, PA. Over the next seven years, Oliver Jr., Margaret, James, and Benjamin were born and their house on King Street was now quite full. Oliver moved from the tannery to the silk mill for a raise in pay. Now that the mills had shut down and the Great Depression was in full swing, Oliver was struggling to know what move to make next. Should he wait and hope the silk mills would settle their disputes with the workers and reopen, or should he move the family again to look for work elsewhere? Estella did not want to leave Stroudsburg so she was placing all her hope in this Coffee Shoppe job.

* * * *

Her first day on the job passed by quickly. There was a lot to learn and many new people to meet. For the breakfast shift, Estella followed an experienced waitress named Louise and marveled at how many customers she could handle at one time without getting things mixed up. Estella hoped that she would be at least half as efficient when the guests for lunch started coming in and she would be assigned her own tables to wait on. Luckily, the lunch crowd was light and the hostess sat customers at only four of her tables. It was good practice, and she left for the day at 3:00 pm feeling confident that the next day – the first day of the busy Memorial Day Weekend – she would do just fine. She even began to daydream about all the tips she hoped to make!

* * * *

"Momma don't go," five-year-old Margaret pleaded and cried as she clung to Estella's skirt at 5:45 am the next morning. "Stay here Momma, don't go to the hotel."

"Oh for heaven's sake, Cricket," Estella comforted her youngest daughter using the pet name she had bestowed on her when she was just a baby. "Momma has to go to work now, but it's just till this afternoon, and then I'll be right back home. Come on now, be a big girl and stop that crying. Can you help your sister with your baby brothers while I'm gone?"

Margaret looked up with tear-streaked cheeks into her mother's smiling eyes and slowly nodded her head yes. Estella walked her to the front window so that Margaret could watch as her mother blew her a kiss then turned and walked down King Street and eventually out of sight.

* * * *

"Oh, thank goodness you're a bit early," the hostess Mildred greeted Estella with exasperation. "Can you do me a favor? The laundry delivered these towels to the Coffee Shoppe, but they belong upstairs for the guest rooms. Could you be a dear and just run them up before you get started with your shift? I'd do it myself, but Mr. McGinn wants to see me in his office right away and I still haven't set up the breakfast juices yet. I'm so behind I think I may go crazy!"

Estella took the stack of towels as she handed her purse to Mildred. This might be a bit more challenging of a day than she had anticipated. Mildred really seemed flustered and the day had not yet begun. Well, at least she was about to see the second floor of the Indian Queen, where she had heard that the guest rooms were quite fancy with the finest of linens and furnishings.

"Right over there, across the lobby, is the door to the staircase, Estella," directed Mildred with a quick glance in the general direction. "At the top of the stairs turn left, then go down to the first housekeeping station on the right. You can't miss it." Mildred turned and all but ran back to the Coffee Shoppe to see what Mr. McGinn needed her for, leaving Estella holding the towels that towered nearly over her head.

Estella crossed the tiled floor of the grand hotel's lobby to a darkened corner where two wooden doors stood side by side. Without even thinking about it, she opened the door on the right, felt for a light switch, but could find none. With the towels stacked in front of her, and very little light, she lifted her leg to begin the climb to the second floor.

The eerie screech of a falling scream immediately brought the front desk attendant running to the staircase.

"Oh my God, Oh my God!" she shouted. "Someone, call Doctor Van der Bie, quick! Oh my God!"

Fellow employees came running to the staircase and quickly realized what had happened. The new waitress from the Coffee Shoppe had tried to deliver a stack of towels to the second floor housekeeping station but mistakenly had opened the door to the cellar instead. In the darkness of the stairwell, and with her vision obstructed by the towels, the pretty young woman had pitched head first down the cellar stairs and was lying lifeless at the bottom. One of the bellhops ran down the stairs and carefully picked Estella up, carrying her gently back up the staircase. The hotel manager was on the phone to Dr. Van der Bie, and the hotel desk clerk had grabbed smelling salts from the first aid kit behind the desk. She quickly tried to revive Estella by waving the ammonia coated salts under her nose but they were having no effect.

Estella's fellow workers stayed with her for what seemed like forever until finally Dr. Van der Bie came running through the front doors of the hotel, medical bag in hand.

"Stand back," he instructed as he quickly knelt down beside Estella to begin his examination. He lifted her eyelids, felt for her pulse, listened to her heartbeat and counted her respirations. Just as he reached to feel under her head, bright red blood began to trickle out of her nose.

"She's unconscious and appears to have fractured her skull," he spoke to the gathering crowd. "Has anyone summoned the ambulance?"

"Yes Doctor, it's on the way," the desk clerk replied as she wiped tears from her eyes.

When the ambulance arrived, Estella was placed on a canvas gurney and loaded into the back, headed for East Stroudsburg General Hospital.

Estella Rarick Nordmark and Her First Child, May

CHAPTER TWO

A Family's Heartbreak

"Yes? Can I help you?" asked ten-year-old May as she peeked through the open crack of the front door of the Nordmark's rental house.

It was a little after 9 o'clock in the morning and May had just finished cleaning up the breakfast of bread and jam she had prepared for her brothers and sister.

"Oh, Pastor Ferguson, come in," May smiled as she opened the door in welcome.

"Is your father at home, May?" Pastor Ferguson asked as he held his hat at his chest, eyes downcast.

"Yes, he's upstairs. I'll go and get him," her voiced trailed off as she ascended the wooden staircase to the second floor. As she reached the top step, she stopped and glanced back downstairs, wondering briefly why Pastor Ferguson looked so sad.

"Father!" May called into her parents' bedroom. "Pastor Ferguson is here to see you."

Oliver opened the door to his room as he fastened the last few buttons of his shirt.

"Pastor Ferguson? What's he want comin' here on a Saturday?" he whispered to May as he raked his fingers through his curly hair.

15

"I dunno," May shrugged her shoulders as she went to her own room to dress for the day.

Oliver went downstairs and extended his right hand in greeting. He knew right away from the look on the Pastor's face that something was terribly wrong.

"Oliver," began Pastor Ferguson. "I'm afraid I have very bad news. I've just come from the General Hospital. It seems that Estella took a tumble down the stairs over at the Indian Queen this morning."

"What? And she's in the hospital?" Oliver asked as he hustled for his boots and jacket. "I've got to get over there!"

"Oliver, wait," spoke Pastor Ferguson as Oliver turned from the door to face him. "Oliver, I'm so sorry but.....She's gone, Oliver. They couldn't revive her. The doc says it was a fractured skull. Chances are, she never knew what happened."

Oliver slunk to the floor in disbelief. With his elbows on his knees, he buried his face in his forearms as he choked back the tears that desperately wanted to fall from his eyes. He tried hard to wrap his brain around what the Pastor had just told him. How could Estella be gone? No, she'll be back just after 3:00 pm when her shift has ended. The Indian Queen Hotel – he *knew* he should never have agreed to let Estella go to work there. This was his fault. He knew that almost right away. *He* should have been the one at work today, not the mother of his six children. Oh dear

16

God, he thought to himself. How on Earth would he and his children get by without Estella? Slowly Oliver stood with his back leaning against the wall for support.

"Would you drive me to the hospital?" Oliver asked the Pastor. "I want to see her."

"Certainly," replied Pastor Ferguson. "I can help you make the arrangements as well, if you'd like."

"Yes, that would be good. I don't know what needs to be done," spoke Oliver in barely a whisper.

Oliver walked to the staircase and called for May to come downstairs and stay with the other children, explaining that he would be back shortly.

"Okay, Father," May said with a questioning look. "Is everything alright?"

"I'll be back shortly, May," was all he could say. "I'll be back shortly."

* * * *

Oliver traveled with Pastor Ferguson to the General Hospital in East Stroudsburg in silence. He was able to sit with Estella for a short time before the doctor came in to offer his condolences and to ask who Oliver would like to handle the funeral arrangements. Pastor Ferguson suggested the funeral home of J. H. Lanterman and Sons and Oliver agreed. From the hospital, Pastor Ferguson drove Oliver to the home of Estella's mother,

Emma Rarick, to share the heartbreaking news. Emma Rarick was a strong, proud woman who had survived many difficult times, including the death of her husband when Estella was just five years old. Much to Oliver's relief, she stepped in and took control of the situation. She traveled with Oliver back to the house on King Street and shared the sad news with her grandchildren, comforting them as their tears flowed.

The afternoon paper, THE RECORD, carried news of the tragedy:

FALL IN HOTEL IS FATAL TO WOMAN
Wife of East Stroudsburg Silk Worker Pitches Into the Cellar

Her husband, a silk worker, out of work and unable to provide for her self and six small children, Mrs. Stella Nordmark wife of Oliver Nordmark of 26 King Street East Stroudsburg, yesterday obtained a job as waitress in the coffee shop of the Indian Queen Hotel.

This morning shortly after 6 o'clock she opened a door to go to the second floor of the hotel but instead she opened a door to the cellar, lost her balance, pitched forward and landed at the foot of the cellar steps. Fellow employees picked her up and called Dr. R. Van Der Bie who found her unconscious and had her removed immediately to the General Hospital where she died at 8:20 from a fractured skull.

G.E. McGinn, manager of the Indian Queen hotel, stated that very little was known at the hotel as to how the accident happened except that it is thought she opened the wrong door and in the dark, did not notice that the steps went down instead of up.

Yesterday the woman, who was only 26 years of age, applied for a position as waitress in the coffee shop and told Mr. McGinn that her husband had been out of work for some time and that there were children to be supported and that if she could get a job they would be able to manage until her husband could again get work.

Mr. McGinn gave her the position and she worked yesterday and returned this morning. She was getting ready to go to work when the accident happened. The remains were taken to the funeral parlor of J.H. Lanterman and Sons, East Stroudsburg.

On Tuesday, May 27th, Oliver was surprised to see a fellow worker from the silk mill at the front door. John Schultz, along with every other mill worker, had been laid off when workers had tried to unionize. Now he stood at Oliver's door with a letter in his hand.

"Come in John, come in," Oliver motioned as he led John to the sofa in the front room.

John was at a loss for words, so he handed Oliver the letter in his hands. It was a "Resolution of Sympathy" that the men had drawn up in support of Oliver due to his sudden loss.

"It's the least we could do, Oliver," John began. "And we chose six of our members to serve as pall bearers tomorrow."

Oliver looked up at his friend and thanked him.

"At the meeting last night we got some good news, Oliver. We received our Charter for a local branch of the United Textile Workers Union, so now we're affiliated with the American Federation of Labor. That means we'll have some serious bargaining power with the mill owners. I'd say we'll all be back to work in no time," John tried to sound optimistic.

"Well, I'd say that's just a little too late for me, John. I sure woulda liked to've heard that about a week ago," sighed Oliver. "Then I never would've told Estella she could go for that job at the Indian Queen."

John lowered his head, not knowing how to reply.

* * * *

On Wednesday morning, the funeral home brought Estella's plain, pinewood casket into the house on King Street and set it on a raised platform in the front room. The funeral director slowly raised the casket lid for viewing. Estella wore a simple green dress and white shoes. Emma, her mother, again took charge of the situation. She brought each of the children to see their mother one last time, lifting the smaller children up so that they could see in the casket.

At 2:00 pm, with guests seated around the living room, Pastor Ferguson gave a brief eulogy, prayed for Estella and the family she left behind, then led the gathering as they sang *Amazing Grace.* Afterward, the casket was taken to Prospect Cemetery where Estella was laid to rest in an unmarked plot.

Returning to their home on King Street, Oliver and his children were emotionally spent from the sad events of the day. As they approached the ramshackle dwelling, Oliver noticed the figures of two finely dressed people near the front door. He approached them with apprehension.

"Can I help you?" he asked with worry in his voice.

"Mr. Nordmark?" inquired the gentleman as he removed his bowler hat.

Oliver gathered his children around him – May holding one-year-old Benny, Oliver Jr., Bud, Margaret and Jim. He wondered if this might be a lawyer or some other official, coming to evict them from their house since the rent was past due and June's rent would be due in just a week.

"Oh Bernard!" the woman gasped as she touched the elbow of what Oliver decided must be her husband. "Look at the baby, he's so sweet!"

She tipped her head to one side pointing at little Benny with her elegantly gloved hand. Her high heels and silk dress told Oliver that she was a woman of means, quite used to getting everything she wanted. As she tried to reach out to touch Oliver's youngest son, May instinctively took a protective step backwards and Oliver tightened his grip on Jim and Margaret.

"Yes, well, allow us to introduce ourselves," the gentleman extended his hand to Oliver. "I am Bernard Levinstein and this is my wife Judith. We have been staying at the Indian Queen for the holiday weekend where we read about your wife's terrible accident. Please accept my condolences."

"Thank you," replied Oliver with skepticism in his voice.

Bernard Levinstein continued with what he and his wife considered a perfectly logical proposal. "When we read in the paper about your circumstances, being out of work and with six children to care for, we realized that we had to help. So we've come to offer to take the baby off your hands. As you can see, we have the means to care for the child and we have no children of our own. I own my own business and have extensive investments to see us through this period of depression that the country is experiencing. He will have a life of privilege," Bernard Levinstein concluded his petition with a smile of satisfaction.

Oliver, on the other hand, became filled with grief-stricken rage. His face flushed as he felt the anger come over him. It took all of his strength to muster the self-control not to knock this man flat on his backside – fancy suit and all. "Over my dead body!" Oliver said with scorn. "These are my children and they'll be stayin' with me. No one is splitting up my family. We just come now from buryin' their mother, Mr. Levinstein, and you have the nerve to be waitin' here at my front door with your offer of 'help'? Well you can just help yourself away from my front door," an indignant Oliver said as he pushed past the couple and shepherded his children into the house.

"But surely you will reconsider," Mr. Levinstein persisted. "A wonderful life in Chicago, attendance at the finest schools, inclusion in the circles of high society – it's far more than you will ever be able to give the child."

"You can't take any of that to the grave, now can you?" Oliver turned and spoke over his shoulder. "These are Nordmark children, and they'll be Nordmarks till the day they die." With that, Oliver slammed the door shut leaving the Levinsteins looking helplessly at one another.

Judith Levinstein looked to her husband, expecting him to right what she perceived as this terrible wrong, but he only shrugged his shoulders. Taking matters into her own hands, she reached up and pounded on the wooden door. Oliver opened the door just a crack.

"Mr. Nordmark, he's just a baby," she pleaded. "He'll never even remember you, or this horrid start to his life."

A disgusted Oliver narrowed his eyes in anger at this stranger's appalling statement. "We'd remember *him*," was his reply, which said it all.

The front door slammed for the final time and the Levinsteins, resigning themselves to failure, turned and began the short walk back to town.

*   *   *   *

Oliver was stunned by the audacity of the Levinsteins. Thinking back to his own childhood, he remembered the terrible feeling of being separated from his brother and sister when they had been sent to an orphanage after their mother's death. Oliver had managed to make the best of the situation, but he knew that their time apart had been ruinous for his brother Edward. He had to try and keep his family together at all costs.

The next day, Oliver called May to the kitchen to instruct her on his plan. He had his .22 rifle on the table, and she was startled as she came down the stairs and saw it lying there.

"What's going on?" she cautiously asked her father.

"May, I'm gonna teach you how to protect yourself and your brothers and sister in case I'm not home," Oliver began. "You need to learn how to handle this rifle since you're the oldest."

Oliver picked up the .22 and led May to the front door. He demonstrated to his daughter how to load the gun, hold it properly, aim, and gently squeeze the trigger. May was not the least bit interested in learning how to handle the firearm, but she dutifully listened to her father hoping that she would never need the skills he imparted.

"Now May, if you're here in charge and someone knocks on the door, I want you to get the gun ready. Shout through the door asking who it is, and if they don't answer, let 'em know you got a gun and ya know how to use it," Oliver told the frightened ten-year-old. "If they don't answer you, just pull the trigger."

May was terrified. "Pull the trigger?" she asked. "Are you sure I should shoot the gun?"

"If they won't answer, and you've given 'em fair warning, then yes, pull the trigger," Oliver confirmed. "We gotta protect our own."

May took her father's instructions to heart, secretly hoping that she would never need to go anywhere near the rifle. Unbeknownst to May, Oliver's lesson in self-protection was not yet complete. Later the following week, Oliver decided to test his daughter to see if his words had taken root in her mind. While she was home alone with her siblings and not expecting her father back for several more hours, Oliver knocked loudly on the front door. May jumped from her seat, her head quickly turning towards the front door.

"Quiet!" she instructed her sister and brothers.

No one spoke a word as May rose from her seat and tip-toed towards the front door. She quietly picked up the rifle that leaned against the table to the right of the door and loaded it. Just as she finished, there was a second loud knock on the door.

"Who's there?" May asked as her voice quivered and her hands shook. There was no reply. "I said who's there?" May shouted this time, hoping beyond hope that the person would answer. Again, there was no response.

"I got a gun here, and I know how to use it," May yelled, hardly believing that the words were coming out of her own mouth. Was she really going to shoot the gun, she asked herself? Her knees felt like they were going to give out on her as she positioned herself in front of the door, gun raised, heart racing.

"Shoot, May," Bud whispered to his sister as he corralled the other children towards the far side of the room.

May glanced in the direction of Bud's voice, then quickly returned her attention to the front door. As she heard a third knock on the door followed by a jiggling of the handle, she knew she had to do it. Closing her eyes tight, May squeezed the trigger as her father had taught her.

"Bang!"

Almost immediately she heard a key in the lock and the door swung open. Oliver, who had been standing off to one side of the door, entered the room full of pride.

"You done the right thing," he congratulated his

daughter who was visibly shaking, the rifle dropped to her side. "You done just what I told you!"

May, regaining her composure, was furious and began yelling at her father. "It was you?" she screamed. "How could you do that? We were terrified!" May glanced back at her brothers and sister who were just as surprised as she was.

Oliver ignored her anger and continued his praise. "It's just what I taught you to do," he smiled with pride. "Now I know you can handle the gun like I told you. I won't test you again, so if it happens again, you'll know it's the real thing and you won't be near as scared," he reasoned to his daughter. "I'm real proud of you."

May, who was still furious, stormed upstairs leaving her father wondering what the problem was. Oliver cocked his head to one side as his gaze followed May up the stairs, then he locked the front door and went to join his other children.

Benny, Jim, Margaret, Oliver, Jr., Bud, & May on King Street

CHAPTER THREE

The Games Children Play

May, Bud, and Oliver Jr. returned to finish out the school year the Monday following their mother's funeral. Emma, their grandmother, made the decision to move in with the family to care for the children while Oliver continued to try to find work. Eventually the labor disputes at the silk mills were settled and workers were called back on a part-time basis, affording Oliver at least a partial income to keep the family fed. The children, although saddened by the loss of their mother, began to return to their youthful exuberance, playing games and getting into childhood mischief. One new and unusual game that they created was called "Playing Funeral".

"Look!" cried four-year-old Jim to his brothers and sisters as they played in the dirt behind the house. It was late June, 1930 and school was out for the summer. "It's a dead grasshopper."

"Wait right there, Jim," Margaret replied. "I'll go and get a matchbox." She ran in the back door of the house and returned quickly with an empty matchbox big enough to hold the grasshopper.

With a large stick, Oliver Jr. started digging in the dirt underneath a distant tree. "I'll dig the grave over here," he shouted to Margaret and Jim.

"Under this tree is a nice place for him."

Margaret gently tucked the dead grasshopper into the matchbox, sliding the lid closed. Leading the procession, followed closely by Jim, she shouted to her eight-year-old brother Bud. "Bud, get in line!" But Bud was having no part of it.

"I'm not playing that stupid game," he called back to Margaret. "Just squash the darn thing!" He folded his arms and turned away in disgust.

Margaret lifted her chin indignantly and continued her procession. By this time little Benny, who was almost one-and-a-half, had curiously fallen in behind Jim as he dragged his tattered blanket through the dirt. Margaret hummed softly as the three reached the shade of the tree.

Oliver Jr. cleared his throat as he stood up pretending to hold a Bible. "We gather today underneath this tree to remember the life of Mr. Grasshopper," he began his sermon. "He lived a good life in the field behind our house, but now it is his time to go to heaven with God and Jesus. Would anyone like to say anything?"

"All the other grasshoppers will miss him," chimed in Margaret.

"His wife grasshopper will miss him," added Jim.

"Lets all sing," instructed Oliver Jr.

Jim, Margaret and Oliver Jr. sang their way through *Jesus Loves Me* as best they could remember it, and then stood quietly for a few seconds as they looked down at the matchbox.

Oliver Jr. then placed the matchbox in the hole he had dug and Margaret knelt down to cover the box with loose dirt, packing it tightly. She ran a few feet away and picked a dandelion to place on top of the grave.

"Good-bye Mr. Grasshopper," Jim said.

With that, the funeral game ended, and the children ran off chasing each other around the yard.

*   *   *   *

Bud, who was almost nine years old, had other ideas about what "fun" was. He had no time for funeral games and spent his summer up on the hill behind the house on King Street. The hill was covered in tall grasses and Bud would sneak his father's .22 rifle out of the house and head for the top of the hill. Quietly he would crouch down among the grasses and wait patiently for the sounds of small creatures. He practiced shooting at squirrels, rabbits, chipmunks, and even snakes. At first he had very few successes, but by mid-summer he could hit just about anything he aimed at. One day, it was almost his brother. As Bud lay hidden in the grass, he quietly listened for sounds that would signal movement, his finger at the ready on the trigger. A rustling sound from behind caught his ear and as he rolled around to shoot, he stopped just in time. Six-year-old Oliver Jr. had wandered up the hill and was headed towards Bud about thirty feet away.

"Oliver!" Bud yelled. "Ya tryin' to get yourself killed or what? What are ya doing up here anyway?"

Oliver Jr. smiled at his big brother not realizing just how narrowly he had escaped a catastrophe. He started to run towards Bud, his wispy blond hair bouncing with each step. As he came closer, he saw the gun and gave Bud a puzzled look.

"What are ya doin' with Dad's gun, Bud?" he asked innocently.

Bud thought fast. "Now that's a secret, don't ya know? But I guess you're big enough to be in on the secret – that is, if you want to be in on it."

"I'm big enough!" Oliver Jr. replied anxiously.

"Well," began Bud as he tried to make something up fast. "Do ya remember how Dad told us that story about when he was a kid in Kansas, and he was such a great shot with a .22? Remember how he said he could shoot a matchstick out of his friend's hand? Well, I'm workin' on a surprise for Dad."

"What kind of surprise?" wondered little Oliver.

"I've been practicing my shot up here on the hill all summer and as soon as I'm as good as Dad, I'm gonna show him what I learned," Bud shared with his brother. "But you can't tell him because that would ruin the surprise, okay?"

"Hmm," thought Oliver Jr. "That's a pretty

good surprise. Can I surprise him too?"

It wasn't what Bud had in mind, but to keep the secret and therefore the ability to continue practicing his shot, he agreed to let his brother come along on his secret escapades. For the rest of the summer, Bud and Oliver Jr. would eagerly look for opportunities to sneak up the hill and work on their surprise. Oliver Jr. was quick to praise his older brother every time a shot hit its target. By the end of the summer, it was safe to say that Bud Nordmark rarely missed his mark.

"Well," Bud thought to himself. "I guess it's like the saying goes, *like father, like son.*"

Infirmary, State Sanatorium, Mont Alto, Pa.

Mont Alto Sanatorium

CHAPTER FOUR

Mont Alto Sanatorium

In the fall of 1930, the four oldest Nordmark children were preparing to return to school. With so little money, there would be no new school clothes this year, and no new shoes either. Oliver was trying to provide for his family, but it was becoming increasingly difficult. When Bud pointed out to his father that the soles on their shoes had worn thin – and in fact were starting to get holes in them – Oliver traveled to the five and dime store in Stroudsburg and purchased four shoe repair kits. Each kit came with a set of rubber soles and some special glue. Oliver cut the rubber soles to match the bottoms of each child's shoes, then applied the glue and had each child stand in their shoes until the glue dried. This fix was effective at first, but after several weeks the front ends of the new soles became loose and flapped when the children walked. They adapted well, and soon learned how to flip their feet upwards when they walked to avoid stumbling over the loose soles.

Near the end of September, Emma Rarick answered a knock at the front door and was surprised to see a gentleman in a suit and top hat standing there with Bud and Oliver Jr. on either side of him. Her first thought was that the boys had gotten themselves into trouble at school but that was not the case.

"Good afternoon," the gentleman began. "My name is Mr. Sandson from the Pennsylvania Department of Health. May I come in?"

"Certainly," a worried Emma replied as she stepped back and allowed the three to enter the house.

"I've just come from the schoolhouse where the Department of Health has conducted a screening of the schoolchildren for tuberculosis. It has been determined that young Francis and Oliver here may in fact be victims of this highly contagious disease based on their height, weight and the pallor of their skin. The department would like to remove them immediately to the Pennsylvania State Sanatorium at Mont Alto for observation, with your permission of course. Should you refuse your permission, we will be forced to quarantine the entire household until we can confirm or deny the suspicion."

Emma Rarick was stunned, and frightened as well. She knew the dangers of tuberculosis as well as many other highly contagious diseases. In fact, when he was just seven years old, Bud had been quarantined with Rheumatic Fever and nearly died while visiting his Aunt Mary's house. May and Oliver Jr. had been sick too and Dr. Van Der Bie had repeatedly painted their throats with iodine. Emma quickly gave her permission to Mr. Sandson and allowed him to take the boys with him immediately. He assured her that they would be in good hands and that the fresh air and sunshine of Mont Alto, along with a good diet and long periods of rest, would lead to a quick recovery. In the meantime, the family would receive monthly updates of their care and progress.

Later that afternoon, when Oliver came home from work, Emma shared with him the news of the Health Department's visit.

"And you let him take the boys, just like that?" he questioned his mother-in-law angrily. "Without my approval?"

"I'm their grandmother, Oliver. I didn't think I needed your approval. Would you prefer to have the whole house quarantined?" Emma shot back at Oliver. "That would include you too you know. So how would we eat then, with no money coming in at all?"

Oliver knew that she was right, but he still wished he had been there when the boys were brought home from school. He realized that there was nothing he could do but wait for the first 'Letter of Care and Progress' to arrive from Mont Alto.

* * * *

"Where are we headed?" a suspicious Bud asked Mr. Sandson as they approached the train station.

"You'll be traveling together to the Mont Alto Sanatorium, Francis," replied Mr. Sandson in a friendly tone. "It is a beautifully scenic place on the top of a mountain where you'll get plenty of fresh, clean air and radiant sunshine."

"Fresh air and sunshine," a skeptical Bud replied. "Don't sound like much of a treatment plan to me. And what's this disease you say we got again? I feel just fine, I'll tell ya that."

"Tuberculosis," answered Mr. Sandson. "It is difficult to diagnose and sometimes even more difficult to treat but don't you worry, you'll be in the best of hands. The doctors at Mont Alto are the best in the country, and they are establishing new and innovative ways of treating even the sickest of patients."

"Yeah, whatever," Bud shrugged as the car came to a halt in front of the loading platform of the train station. "I guess it'll be more excitin' than school, anyway."

Mr. Sandson left the boys in the car while he went to the window to purchase the tickets. He returned as the boys were climbing out of the car and explained what would happen next.

"Now I'm going to pin a string of tickets onto each of your jackets," he began as he reached for Oliver Jr.'s collar. "The conductor will come to you at each stop along the way and remove one ticket," he continued as he moved along to Bud's jacket collar. "When he removes your last ticket, that will be your stop at Mont Alto and there will be a nurse to meet you when you disembark from the train."

"How long will we be on the train?" whispered Oliver Jr., just a little frightened.

"Oh it won't take long at all," Mr. Sandson assured him. "You'll have a pleasant ride and arrive later this evening - probably in time for supper."

The boys loaded onto the train along with the other waiting passengers and took a seat just inside the door.

"Good-bye!" waved a smiling Mr. Sandson.

"Good-bye," the boys waved hesitantly as they settled in for the journey.

* * * *

Bud and Oliver Jr. took turns sharing the window seat as they traveled along towards Franklin County, Pennsylvania. The further along they rode, the more beautiful the scenery became. By late afternoon, the conductor had removed all but one of their string of tickets. The boys began to feel the train going up, up, up as it wound around many curves.

"Feels like we're climbing a mountain," observed Oliver Jr. to his big brother.

Bud leaned across the seat and peered out the window. "It doesn't just feel like it, Oliver, we are climbin' a mountain, I'd say."

It was nearly dusk when the boys heard the

train whistle blow and the conductor came and removed their last ticket.

"This here's your stop boys," he said as he took a step backwards. "No tickets left."

As the train rumbled to a stop, spewing big clouds of black smoke from the engine, the boys made their way out of their seats to the side door. When it was completely stopped, they opened the door and jumped down to the platform and took a good look around. What they saw was a beautiful sight. They were surrounded by a lush green forest of trees and the air was sweetly scented. They saw a woman in a nurse's cap approaching them.

"Welcome boys," she smiled. "I will escort you to the Sanatorium and get you checked in. If we hurry, you'll be just in time for supper."

On the short ride from the train station to the Sanatorium, the nurse explained to the boys just what lay ahead for them.

"Mont Alto is a state-of-the-art facility established by the Pennsylvania Department of Health for the treatment of tuberculosis patients," she knowingly began. "It encompasses six hundred and fifty acres smack dab in the middle of fifty-five thousand acres of state forestlands. We have approximately eleven hundred patients at any given time housed in small cottages of eight people. You boys may be able to stay in the same cottage."

Bud and Oliver Jr. glanced at each other and smiled. They felt just fine, so they started to get a bit excited about this adventure. They could really have some fun on six hundred and fifty acres!

* * * *

Unfortunately for the boys, "fun" was not on the daily schedule at the Mont Alto Sanatorium. The treatment for suspected tuberculosis in the 1930's was a regimen of fresh air, sunlight, a healthy diet and long periods of inactivity to rest the lungs. Patients, including Bud and Oliver Jr., were forced to spend long periods of time outside on reclining chairs, whatever the weather. They also attended classes where they were taught proper hygiene with an emphasis on the cessation of the bad habit of spitting. This was thought to be a major cause of the spread of many diseases, particularly tuberculosis, or TB, as it was commonly called.

The boys quickly became bored with doing the same thing day after day and spending a lot of time just sitting around. They began to look forward to the time when they could go home again. As the weather got colder and winter arrived, Oliver Jr. was sent to the infirmary with a sore throat on three separate occasions. The doctors decided in February that he must have tonsillitis and they quickly scheduled him to have his tonsils removed.

"It's just a sore throat," Oliver Jr. pleaded with the doctor. "Probably from all that time I gotta spend sittin' outside doin' nothing. I don't see why I need an operation for a sore throat."

"Now you just leave that decision to us," the doctor reassured him. "You won't feel a thing and it will serve to improve your overall health."

The day of the operation, Oliver Jr. was instructed to change into a hospital gown and was wheeled on a narrow table into a small room with lots of bright lights. The doctor placed an ether mask over his nose and mouth and instructed Oliver Jr. to breathe in deeply ten times. Oliver Jr. was frightened as he took a deep breath of the bad smelling gas. By the end of his second breath, he was unconscious.

"Oliver!" a young nurse called to him. "Oliver, wake up now. Your operation is over."

Oliver Jr. was very groggy and lightheaded as he slowly came to. He saw the nurse's face wave in and out of his line of vision and he felt as though he might throw up. As soon as he became more coherent, he realized that his throat felt like it was on fire.

"Now don't try to talk," the nurse silenced him as she placed her hand on his shoulder. "You're going to have some pain in your throat for a few days but I'll give you some medicine that will help with that."

Oliver Jr. just closed his eyes and drifted back to sleep as he wondered who in the world thought *this* was the "cure" for a sore throat!

* * * *

Within a few weeks, Oliver Jr. was feeling better from his tonsillectomy. He was still being kept in the hospital of the sanatorium so he hadn't seen his brother in quite awhile and was beginning to feel homesick for the first time. When the mail arrived later that day, the delivery brought a smile to his face.

"Mail for you, Oliver," his nurse smiled as she handed him a package.

With great excitement, Oliver Jr. tore into the small package that was postmarked from East Stroudsburg and addressed in what he presumed was his father's hand. Inside he found a handmade Valentine card from his sister May and a small box of little red heart-shaped candies.

"Oh Oliver," his nurse frowned as she reached for the box. "You can't have candy. It's not on the special diet here at the sanatorium. Let me take that." She reached for the box which Oliver Jr. reluctantly handed over to her with a face so sad she thought he might cry.

"I'll tell you what," she conspired with him. "I'll give you two pieces if you promise not to tell anyone."

"You got a deal," he agreed as he reached out his hand.

The young nurse secretly opened the small box and placed two tiny candies in Oliver's hand. Then she smiled at him, turned away and ate the rest of the box herself!

* * * *

By spring of 1931, Oliver Jr. and Bud were released from Mont Alto Sanatorium to return to their family in East Stroudsburg. It was determined by the doctors that, in fact, neither one had ever had tuberculosis but that the fresh air and healthy food had done both of them some good. They had gained a little weight and their color was improved.

Returning home, the boys were eagerly greeted by their brothers and sisters and by their father and grandmother. They quickly melted back into their old routines of going to school and getting into mischief. They enjoyed chasing the trains to see who could run the furthest, and they took turns seeing who could swipe a treat from the Bakery Wagon as it traveled down King Street towards town. Every now and then they played hooky from school, spending the day skipping rocks on a nearby creek. It was good to be home!

CHAPTER FIVE

Boys Will Be Boys!

As the summer of 1931 began in the Nordmark household, Oliver found it hard to believe that his wife Estella had been gone for an entire year. A wrongful death lawsuit had been filed against the Indian Queen Hotel on behalf of Estella's children, but the case had not yet been brought to court and there was no telling how long it might take. Oliver was still working part-time hours at the silk mill but wages were low and getting by each day was a financial struggle. Still, Oliver tried to keep his spirits up to make sure that his children were not burdened by his worries. There was no evidence that the boys, at least, were worried by anything and their grandmother, Emma Rarick, was beginning to reach her wits end with their antics, as well as the emotional and physical struggle of caring for six young children at her age.

"Jim!" she yelled to her five-year-old grandson as he played outside on the sidewalk one early summer morning. "Come over here this instant. Now how many times have I told you this bedwetting has got to stop?" She shook a wet bed sheet at little Jim and her face crinkled in anger. "I don't have time, with all you kids, to be washing sheets every day, do you hear me?" She took Jim

Emma Rarick

by the arm and led him to the front stoop of the house where there was an enclosed cubbyhole behind the steps with a latticework door that locked. Emma gave Jim a push into the cubbyhole then threw the wet sheet in on top of his head and shut the door. "Now just stay in there with that sheet until you make up your mind to stop this bedwetting once and for all!" She stomped up the stairs into the house, leaving Jim to cower in the corner of the cubbyhole in fright.

As she entered the house, Emma realized that she didn't see her youngest grandson Benny anywhere, and in fact, hadn't seen him for some time.

"May!" she shouted for Oliver's oldest daughter. "May, where has Benny gotten to?"

"I don't know," replied May innocently as she lifted her head from the book she was reading at the kitchen table. "I thought he was outside with Jim."

"Jim's busy learning a lesson under the front steps. Now put that book down and help me find Benny," Emma scolded May as she took the book from her hands and dropped it on the table.

May reluctantly left her seat and looked out the back door for little Benny. She didn't see him anywhere so she left the house and started to climb the hill out back, calling his name. Emma checked upstairs to no avail then followed May out back, checking on either side of the house. The sound of a long, low whistle and billowing black smoke rising from the far side of King Street signaled the arrival of an incoming freight train, causing Emma to stand frozen in her tracks. Could the happy-go-lucky toddler have wandered down to the railroad tracks?

"Oh God, no," Emma whispered to herself as she hurried around to the front of the house, down the sloping front yard and across King Street. She struggled to make it down a slight embankment just as the train's caboose passed by. Along the side of the tracks, smiling and waving to the train, was little Benny. He started to run towards his Grammy who was still trying to climb down the hill.

"Hi Grammy!" Benny waved with a grin.

Emma took the young boy in her arms as her heart stopped racing and she silently thanked God that he was safe. "What are you doing down here?" she finally managed to ask.

"I came to see the trains," Benny replied. "They wave to me. And that lady and that man gives me candy. They nice to me."

Emma looked beyond the street to a small house where an older couple sat on the front porch rockers. She realized then that she had been lax in her tending of this small child. Clearly Benny knew this couple as they smiled and waved up at him in Emma's arms. How long had he been visiting them, she wondered? How could she not have missed him previously? Remembering that the other children were unattended back at the house, Emma gathered up two-and-a-half-year-old Benny and headed back towards King Street. When she reached the front step, she bent down and unlocked the cubby door, her heart heavy with regret, knowing that she was not capable of continuing to care for six small children.

* * * *

"Oliver, you have got to do something about these boys and their behavior," Emma Rarick confronted Oliver as he walked through the door at the end of the workday. "Something bad is going to happen, I can just feel it. They're forever getting into trouble and I don't know how much longer this can go on."

"They're just being boys, Emma," Oliver smiled as he remembered some of the things he and his brother had done as boys growing up in Kansas. "What could happen?"

"What could happen? I'll tell you what could happen!" Emma replied with a tone of warning. "Benny could get run over by the train, that's one thing that could happen. I found him down by the tracks today. And just yesterday I caught Bud and Oliver Jr. headed out the back door with that rifle of yours planning to do God knows what! Someone could get killed, that's what could happen, Oliver!"

Oliver just smiled and carried his lunch pail to the kitchen. These were not things to worry about as far as he was concerned. The boys would be fine, he was sure of that.

Emma rolled her eyes at what she perceived as disinterest from Oliver and headed in frustration to the backyard to remove the morning wash from the clothesline.

* * * *

"Dad!" yelled May coming through the front door. "Come quick! Benny's in your car and it's rolling forward!"

Oliver ran for the front door, knocking over a kitchen chair in his path. Outside he saw his old jalopy drifting towards the road with little Benny standing up in the driver's seat.

"Benny!" he yelled as he ran for the car, his heart pounding. Oliver raced out into the street and reached for the car's door handle, yanking it open. He shoved Benny aside and jumped in, slamming the brake just in time. Oliver had brought the car to a halt just before it tumbled down the embankment towards the railroad tracks.

"Drive!" Benny smiled as he looked up at his dad. "Drive the car!"

"Yeah, you drove the car alright," Oliver smiled as he took a deep breath, calming his pulse. Boys will be boys, Oliver thought to himself, but that was a close one. He gathered Benny up in his arms and carried him into the house, then returned to park the car on more level ground.

As he walked back inside, Oliver knew he was going to hear from Emma about this.

"You see what I mean?" Emma spoke in a knowing tone as she walked past Oliver. "These kids are out of control. And all you can say is, 'boys will be boys'."

* * * *

Late in the summer of 1931, Oliver's sons had their last adventure in the care of their Grammy Rarick. Little did they know that their quest for fun was about to alter their world.

"Hey Oliver! Hey Jim!" called Bud to his brothers. "Come on up the hill with me. I want to show you something I figured out!"

The boys bounded up the hill behind their house to the field of tall grass that extended over several acres. It was a sunny day and Bud had secretly brought along his father's magnifying glass, which he had tucked into the pocket of his trousers. Kneeling down in the tall grass, Bud positioned the magnifying glass to reflect the brilliant rays from the sun onto the drying grass.

"Whatcha doin' with that?" asked Oliver Jr. as he looked from the magnifying glass to the sun and back to the glass again.

"Just wait, you'll see," Bud replied as he concentrated on the task at hand.

"Why you makin' the grass look in the magnifying glass?" wondered Jim as he absently pulled at the tall blades that rubbed against his leg.

"It's not the grass, it's the sun," corrected Bud. "Now just watch and be quiet, I'm concentrating."

The boys watched and waited. Just as they were starting to get bored and looking for something else to do, a tiny spark ignited a blade of dry grass.

"Wow! Did ya see that?" an amazed Jim shouted.

"Stand back!" commanded Bud.

Jim and Oliver Jr. obeyed their older brother and within seconds, more grass had flickered into the flame. Before they knew it, a small area of grass was on fire. Bud stood back to admire his work.

"How 'bout that?" he said proudly. "I made fire with no matches!"

The boys stared, mesmerized by the small fire in front of them. What they didn't realize was that it was quickly growing. It was Bud who had the first inkling that this would not end well.

"Stomp it out!" he shouted as he came out of his flame-induced trance. "Come on, help me stomp it out!"

His shouting brought Jim and Oliver Jr. to action as they tried to step on the growing flames. It soon became clear that they were fighting a losing battle. The gentle summer wind blew west, carrying the flames with it. As the boys looked in the direction of the spreading flames, their faces grew with fear. The fire was headed straight down the hill towards the Maplehurst Inn.

"Quick!" shouted Bud. "We gotta get out of here!"

All three boys ran back across the field and down the hill towards their house.

"There's a fire! There's a fire!" shouted Jim as they raced into the house.

"Calm down, now. Where's the fire?" asked Grammy Rarick as she looked past the boys into the backyard.

"Up on the hill, in the field!" answered Oliver Jr. trying to catch his breath. "Bud shined the magnifying glass at the sun and the whole field's caught on fire!"

Emma hurried to the backyard. Looking up towards the field, she shielded her eyes against the bright sunlight. "I don't see a fire in the field," she remarked.

"It's blowin' down the hill to the Maplehurst Inn," Bud admitted in fear. "I gotta go warn them!" He raced out the front door and down King Street, then turned sharply onto North Courtland Street in the direction of the hotel.

Emma brought the other children in the house as she kept a watchful eye up the hill. If the direction of the fire changed, she wanted as much warning as possible to get the family out of harm's way. It seemed like forever, but finally she heard the clanging of the fire engine's bell as the fire department raced towards the Maplehurst Inn and the encroaching flames. An hour later, Bud came through the front door with a satisfied look on his face.

"No need to worry about a thing," he smiled. "All's well that ends well. The fire department came and put out the fire long before it reached the hotel."

"Don't be so smug, Bud," Grammy Rarick admonished the young boy. "Wait till your father gets home and hears about the trouble you've caused!"

When Oliver came home from work later that day, Emma met him at the front door.

"These boys have really done it this time, Oliver!" she began her tirade. "They started the whole field on fire and nearly burnt down the Maplehurst Inn. Lucky thing the fire department got there just in time."

"Started the field on fire? Are you sure?" Oliver asked with a questioning look. "How could they do that?"

"How should I know how they did that? But I tell you they did. Came right in here and admitted it. Then Bud went racing to warn the hotel the flames were headed their way." Emma's whole body shook with the thought of this latest close call. "People could have been killed, Oliver!" she shouted. "Do you hear me? Killed! I've had all I can take of these kids, Oliver. I've tried to help you with keepin' this household running but I'm just too old for all this excitement. My health can't take it any longer. You're going to have to find some other way to take care of these children."

As Emma left the room to pack her belongings, Oliver sat down and held his head in his hands. What would he do now? How was he going to keep his family together without Emma here to keep an eye on things during the day?

"I'll figure something out," he thought to himself. "I always figure something out."

Oliver Nordmark

CHAPTER SIX

The Children's Aid Society

Emma Rarick left Oliver's home that same day, returning to the relative calm and quiet of her son George's home in Corning, New York. Estella's sister Mary and her husband Will tried to help Oliver with the children as often as they could manage, but with a family of their own and limited income, their help could not be counted upon. Oliver struggled along, relying heavily on his oldest daughter May, who at eleven years of age, took on the role of surrogate mother.

By Christmas of that year, Oliver was beginning to realize that he simply didn't have the means to care for his family. The harsh cold of an early winter caused Oliver to run out of fuel for the house much earlier than he had anticipated, with no money to buy more. He tried to make do with burning fires in the fireplace, but it was still quite cold in the house. It was hard for Oliver to watch his children as they huddled near the glowing flames anticipating Santa's arrival in just a week's time, knowing that Santa would not be coming to King Street this year.

On Christmas Eve, the children's faces were full of excitement.

"Santa comes tonight!" Jim announced as he

ran around the living room unable to contain himself. "Tonight's Christmas Eve!"

Benny chimed in as he raced around behind Jim, "Santa! Santa!"

"Now just remember," Oliver said knowingly. "Santa can't always make it to every house. Sometimes he can find your house and sometimes he can't."

The children, however, were not about to believe that. Later that night as they finally became sleepy and drifted off on makeshift beds around the fireplace, their heads were full of the possibilities that the morning might bring.

Oliver sat by himself at the kitchen table as he watched the snow falling outside. He felt terrible about not being able to provide adequately for his children. "If only this hadn't happened. If only Estella were still here and there were still decent jobs to be had," he thought to himself. "This Depression's got the whole country down."

Rising from the table, about to make his way to the sofa where he had been spending his nights to stay warm, Oliver heard a quiet rapping at the front door. He went over and slowly opened it, surprised to see Mary and Will standing in the snowy doorway.

"What are you doing?" Oliver asked in wonderment as Will pushed silently past him, arms full of packages. Mary followed behind him carrying two scooters.

"We ran into Santa Claus, who was extremely

busy, and he asked us if we wouldn't mind delivering these to the Nordmark children," Mary whispered as Oliver looked at her with disbelief.

Mary just smiled as she and Will tip-toed to the living room, leaving their packages by the sleeping children, then headed back towards the front door.

"It's true," Will confirmed. "Just giving Santa a little helping hand. Merry Christmas, Oliver."

As they walked past him and back out the front door, Oliver turned his head to keep them from seeing the tears in his eyes. "Thank you," he managed to say quietly as he closed the door behind them. "Thank you."

* * * *

Christmas morning was filled with surprises as the children awoke to find the gifts that Santa had indeed brought.

"Looks like Santa had no trouble finding our house after all!" a triumphant Jim shouted with excitement.

Oliver smiled as he watched his children enjoying the moment. Oliver Jr. and Bud jumped on the scooters and rode them up and down the room. Oliver wished more than anything that Estella could be here to see them, but he was thankful, at least, that her sister had been so kind.

* * * *

By the middle of January 1932, things had become desperate and Oliver knew what he had to do. In 1854, the Children's Aid Society had been established to help children in need. Oliver and his brother Edward, in fact, had been helped by the Society when their own mother had died. They had first been taken to the Children's Village Orphanage and later sent west on an "orphan train" in search of a home. With the onset of Child Labor Laws in 1929, the "orphan trains" no longer transported children to farms in the Midwest. The Children's Aid Society, however, was still finding ways to help needy children. Oliver found himself thinking more and more about contacting them to see if they could help his children.

The catalyst came as Oliver was about to leave work on Friday, January 29th. As the men were filing past the main office of the silk mill, the foreman stepped out and held up his hand.

"Men, I'm sorry to be the one to have to tell you," he began with a tone of dread. "But this here's the last day of work we can pay anyone for until sometime mid-spring."

A heavy sigh was heard throughout the ranks of the workers as they hung their heads with this latest blow to their survival.

"Now I'm hoping to be able to call some of you back by the end of March," he tried to sound hopeful. "We'll be sending out notices when we know more." He turned and headed back into the office as the men left the mill.

Oliver knew he was finished. He had no savings to carry him over until March and no hopes of finding another job quickly. He left the silk mill and drove his old car straight to the office of the Children's Aid Society.

"I need help with my children," Oliver began as he sat in the Society's office. "You helped me and my brother when we were kids and I'm hoping you can help my six children."

Oliver went on to tell the aid worker, Miss Martin, his entire story. He began with remembering how the Children's Aid Society had tried to help him and his brother back in the early 1900's when they were placed on an orphan train to Kansas in search of a home. He then told her about his wife, Estella, and how they had married young and had six children before her sudden death almost two years ago. He told Miss Martin of his struggles to provide for his children after his mother-in-law left and how with this latest setback of a second layoff at the mill, he just could not see a way to survive.

Miss Martin listened intently to Oliver's tale. She had heard many stories of hardship since the country entered into this depression three years ago but this one in particular tugged at her heartstrings. Even so, she knew there were very few solutions to Oliver's predicament.

"The only thing I can suggest, Mr. Nordmark, is that you place the children in our care," Miss Martin began slowly. "We will put them in a foster home until you can once again provide for them."

Oliver had never felt so defeated in his life. What kind of father, he thought to himself, would give up his children to strangers? He shuffled his feet under the table as he thought about what he should do. Would it be better to keep them all together, going days possibly without enough food to eat? How long could he keep a roof over their heads before the landlord would evict them for not paying the rent, which was already two months past due? Sadly, Oliver came to the realization of what he needed to do.

"Will I know where they are?" questioned Oliver. "Will they be able to stay together in the same home? I don't want them split up."

"Yes," replied Miss Martin gently. "And you will be informed as to their whereabouts at all times and with prior notice, visits can be arranged at the convenience of the foster family."

"It will only be until I can find work again," Oliver assured the aid worker, trying to convince himself, as much as Miss Martin.

"If it will make things any easier, I will go to your home and collect the children and deliver them to the foster family," Miss Martin said sympathetically. "That way there will be no tearful good-byes that may prove difficult for the children. That's usually how we handle situations such as these. It's best for all concerned."

Oliver gave Miss Martin his address on King

Street in East Stroudsburg, then quietly left the office. Once outside, he realized he didn't know what he should do next or where he should go. He thought of Estella, and how disappointed in him she would be. Then his thoughts turned to her sister Mary and he decided to pay her and Will a visit.

* * * *

"Oliver," Mary smiled as she opened the door for her brother-in-law. "What brings you here this time of day?"

"It's bad news, Mary," began Oliver who was suddenly overcome with anguish as the tears fell uncontrollably.

Alarmed, Mary guided Oliver to a chair in the kitchen of her small apartment. "What's happened?" she asked hesitantly, fearful that something had happened to one of Estella's children.

Through sobbing tears, Oliver poured out the events of the day to Mary, concluding with his visit to the Children's Aid Society and the impossible decision he had been forced to make for his children.

Mary tried to comfort him as best she could with consoling words about the difficult times that everyone was facing and how his burden was doubly hard since the loss of his wife.

There was little that Oliver could say in reply.

He could not be consoled right now. He had been forced to make the most painful decision of his thirty-four years and he just couldn't think clearly at the moment.

CHAPTER SEVEN

Adventures in Farm Life

Miss Martin of the Children's Aid Society waited for Oliver to leave her office, then gathered her things and drove to the home of Mr. and Mrs. Oscar Balliet of nearby Saylorsburg to inquire about a temporary home for six small children. The Balliets had added their names to the Society's list of potential foster families with the understanding that they would be paid weekly for each child.

"Six children?" Eva Balliet asked with an eager tone as Miss Martin presented her request at the front door of the Balliets' brick home. "And we get paid for each one?"

"Yes, Mrs. Balliet," Miss Martin assured her. "These are the children you may have read about in the newspaper a few years back. Their mother was killed in an accident at the Indian Queen Hotel and their father has just lost his job and can no longer provide for them."

"Six children," Mrs. Balliet smiled as she added on her fingers. "Yes, we have room for six children."

"Wonderful," a relieved Miss Martin replied. "I'll deliver them later this afternoon. Thank you very much Mrs. Balliet."

* * * *

After returning to her office and completing the necessary paperwork and filings for this newest foster care placement, Miss Martin grabbed her car key and traveled to King Street in East Stroudsburg. With a brief explanation, she unceremoniously gathered up Oliver's children and drove them across town to Saylorsburg.

"When will our father be coming back for us?" asked May as she pondered this latest development.

"It's hard to say for sure," replied Miss Martin vaguely. "Sometimes these situations are resolved quickly, sometimes it takes a little longer."

"Hmm," was May's only response. "Now we're a *situation*," she thought to herself.

Arriving at the Balliets' brick house in Saylorsburg, the children piled out of Miss Martin's car. The boys began roughhousing in the driveway as Miss Martin went to ring the doorbell.

"Boys!" she called from the front step. "Settle down now, you'll want to make a good first impression."

Eva Balliet came out of the house, approaching the six children. She was a large woman who wore her graying black hair pulled back in a sloppy bun. In a firm, loud voice she called out as she approached the driveway.

"Children!" she shouted as she clapped her hands loudly. "Line up, oldest to youngest so I can

66

get a look at you."

Oliver's boys ignored Mrs. Balliet's command but May could see from the corner of her eye that this woman meant business.

"Bud!" called May to her brother. She grabbed his coat, separating him from Oliver Jr., and pulled him into line. The others followed and Margaret found her spot between Oliver Jr. and Jim. Little Benny kept his head lowered as his tiny foot kicked at the gravel driveway.

"Well," announced Mrs. Balliet as she eyed the six children who stood before her. "That's more like it. I expect complete obedience while you are living in this house."

Miss Martin introduced the children to their new foster mother, instructed them to mind their manners and obey Mr. and Mrs. Balliet, then headed towards her car.

"And the first check will arrive by the end of the week?" questioned Eva Balliet as she followed Miss Martin to her car.

"Yes, by the end of the week," Miss Martin replied.

"For all six children, right?" Mrs. Balliet confirmed eagerly.

Miss Martin sighed. "Yes, Mrs. Balliet, for all six children."

"Just so there's no confusion," Mrs. Balliet replied as she cocked her shoulders back and lifted her chin. "Payment for six children."

Miss Martin climbed into her car shaking her

head. If only there was another way, she thought to herself. If only there was another way. She put the car in reverse and backed out of the drive.

* * * *

Oliver's children quickly settled into the routines of the Balliet household. Both of their foster parents were strict and required all of the children to do chores around the house. When warmer weather came, the family moved to their large farm in Cherry Valley about five miles away. In addition to the cottage that the family lived in, there was also a large boarding house that the Balliets rented out to vacationers from New York City. The first thing that Eva Balliet did upon arriving at their farm was to prepare the Spring Tonic for each of the children. This mixture of sulfur and molasses was a popular remedy used to clean out one's system from the ills of winter and prevent infections. As the children lined up for their dose of the Spring Tonic, they turned up their noses.

"Our dad doesn't make us take that stuff," nine-year-old Bud protested.

"Well," Eva Balliet replied with a smirk. "Maybe that's why you're not with your dad right now. So open up and take your Tonic. We don't have time or money for sick children."

Bud decided not to fight this particular battle and opened his mouth to the sulfur and molasses mixture, reminding himself that it was only something they needed to do once a year.

There were many chores to be done on the farm. The Balliets had large truck patches where the children learned their first job.

"All right now children," Eva Balliet instructed all six children as she handed each a small tin can from the shed. It was early morning, just after breakfast, and the children were eager to see what was in store for the day. "This will be a regular chore for all of you, all summer long," Mrs. Balliet began. "If this garden's going to produce enough vegetables for us to eat through next winter, we can't be lettin' potato bugs get at the plants. Hold out your cans."

As each of the children held out their can in front of them, Mrs. Balliet poured a small amount of kerosene in the bottom of each one.

"Now follow me," she instructed as she headed towards the nearest truck patch garden. Arriving at the edge of the garden, which spanned over three hundred square yards, she continued her instruction. "These potato bugs will destroy our vegetables if we don't stay on top of them. Now each of you start in your own row, and hold your can underneath the leaves like this," she demonstrated. "Use your other hand to tap, tap, tap on the top of the leaf to knock the bug into your can where it will drown in the kerosene." She looked up at the children who were just standing and staring as if in a daze. "Well, what are you waiting for?" Eva Balliet asked with a tone of disapproval. "Get to work. This is a big patch and there's two more when this one is finished."

Without further discussion, the children each began at the start of a garden row and quickly got the hang of tapping the potato bugs into their cans. Mrs. Balliet headed off to a nearby pond, leaving the children to work on their own.

"I'm tired," complained three-year-old Benny after completing just half a garden row. He sat down in the dirt and began examining the bugs in his can.

May looked over in Benny's direction and decided not to scold him into action unless she saw Mrs. Balliet coming back from the pond. She certainly didn't want him to bear the brunt of her anger if she found him playing, but he was just a little boy. She put her mind to working as fast as she could to make up for the shortcomings of her youngest brother.

The six children worked late into the morning. They were hot and tired when Bud looked up and noticed Mrs. Balliet headed towards them with two pickerel hanging from the line of her bamboo fishing pole.

"I'm headed up to the house to fry these fish for lunch," she called out to the small workers. "Keep working and I'll call for you when they're ready."

The thought of a meal spurred the children to complete the row each was working in before hearing the call to eat. After lunch, Mrs. Balliet wasted no time assigning the next chore.

"Jim, you go on now and take Benny back to the truck patch with your cans. Margaret, you go along with them too. You other three come along with me to the pond."

"The pond," thought Bud to himself. "Now that should be some fun!"

But fun was not what Eva Balliet had in mind. Climbing into the rowboat that was tied up alongside the small dock, she shouted to the boys who were poking sticks into the lily pads that floated on the water's surface. "Bud, Oliver! Come over here and get in the boat. Bud, you row the oars."

Eager to assume his role as ship's captain, Bud pushed past Oliver and May, nearly jumping into the center of the rowboat.

"May, grab those long handled sickles and that rope and climb in. Oliver, you too," Mrs. Balliet instructed.

After all four people, two long handled sickles, and two coils of rope were loaded into the rowboat, Bud pushed off from the side of the dock and positioned himself to row the oars. It took a little practice to coordinate both arms to move in exactly the same motion, with the same amount of force to enable the boat to go straight, but Bud soon had the rhythm of rowing and they headed for the middle of the large pond.

"Stop here!" shouted Eva Balliet, startling all

three children aboard.

Bud stopped rowing but the boat continued drifting along.

"Stop the boat!" she shouted again. "Push the oars in the opposite direction."

Bud quickly picked up the oars and reversed his rowing which immediately brought the rowboat to a halt. Mrs. Balliet just shook her head as she reached for the ropes lying in the bottom of the boat.

"May, tie this around Oliver's waist," Eva instructed, handing May a length of rope while she picked up a second length and handed it to Bud. "Tie this around your waist, Bud. We need to get to work removing these lily pads."

Bud quickly came to realize just what the purpose of this rowboat ride was. He reached for a long handled sickle and extended it over the side of the boat, whacking at the lily pads.

"Not like that!" yelled Mrs. Balliet. She grabbed the rope and quickly tied it around Bud's waist. "Now, I'll hold the rope and you lower that sickle as far down in the water as you can. Don't cut the lily pad until you're as far down as you can reach. The further down you cut it, the longer it will take to grow back."

Bud did as he was instructed and May did the same on the opposite side of the boat, lowering Oliver Jr. as far down as she dare without dropping him. The lily pad cutting went on for over an hour. It was strenuous work for Bud and Oliver Jr.

as they pushed the sickle against the weight of the water cutting the stems of the lily pads. It was equally as difficult for May and Mrs. Balliet who were tasked with holding the boy's weight to keep them from falling into the pond. By the time Mrs. Balliet decided they could stop for the day, the children were all exhausted.

*　*　*　*

The summer months wore on and the children enjoyed the fresh air and open spaces of farm living. There was lots of work to be done, and Mr. and Mrs. Balliet were not affectionate foster parents, but the children soon adjusted and settled into the expected routines. Every Saturday evening, it was May's job to take her brothers and sister to the pond for their weekly bath. Sundays were spent almost entirely in church services where the preacher, an energetic sort of fellow, would practically run back and forth behind the kneeling rail, shouting the teachings of Jesus and working himself into a near frenzy. Little Benny was so impressed by this passionate display that he could often be found standing on a tree stump preaching loudly to the barnyard animals. On other occasions, he could be found tagging behind Oscar Balliet as he plowed the field. Benny would reach into the loosened soil for artichokes – or arties as they called them – brush off the dirt and enjoy the taste of the crisp and juicy pure white center. By late summer, the children were more than comfortable with knowing what they could, and could not get away with, and they often pushed the boundaries just to see what would happen.

"Oliver!" called out Bud from the barn to his younger brother. "Come and help me get this steer out of the barn."

Oliver Jr. wandered into the barn, followed by Jim and Benny.

"Come on," Bud instigated. "Let's take this guy out for a ride, what do ya say?"

Oliver and Jim coaxed the steer out of the barn with Bud closing the door behind them; or at least he *thought* that he had closed it.

"Climb on and ride him!" an excited Jim told his big brother Bud.

Bud would have loved to try, but the steer was too tall. "I can't get up that high," he pondered as he looked around. "Hey, let's put Benny on for a ride!"

He picked up Benny and plopped him on top of the steer. Startled by the weight suddenly on his back, the animal took off in a panic. Benny instinctively tried to hold on but within a few yards went flying off the back of the steer, landing in the dirt. Running behind, Bud quickly picked up his little brother who was not hurt but was terribly frightened.

"Get the steer!" he yelled to Jim and Oliver Jr. who began chasing after the steer before it could get out of the barnyard. Catching up to it, they grabbed the rope tied around its neck and persuaded it to turn and head back to the barn. As they approached the barn, with Benny riding on Bud's shoulders and Jim and Oliver Jr. leading the steer, Bud realized right away that they now had bigger problems. The door to the barn had not been properly latched and all the sheep were escaping into the adjacent field.

"Aw geez!" shouted Bud taking Benny down from his shoulders. "We're in for trouble now!"

All four boys ran about trying to corral the sheep together to get them back into the barn. At just that moment, Oscar Balliet stepped out from behind the barn on his way to the chicken house.

"What the....?" he shouted as he ran to help the boys.

"Rex!" called Bud to their trusty German Shepherd. "Rex, come!" Rex came running from the front yard and joined the melee as eventually the situation came under control and all the sheep were returned to the barn.

"I don't even *want* to know how that happened," an angry Mr. Balliet scolded the boys. "Just be glad none of them got away or there would have been a price to pay!" With that, he turned and headed towards the chicken house leaving the four boys snickering behind his back.

* * * *

As September drew near, the Nordmark children began to prepare for their return to school. While they lived in Cherry Valley, they would attend The Lower School under the instruction of Hen Fenner. This would be Jim's first year at school and although he was excited, he was also a bit apprehensive.

"Seems like we have to go awfully early," he complained to his sister May as the five of them walked the half mile to the one room schoolhouse. "How long do we have to stay there?"

"We'll be there most of the day Jim," May replied. That's why Mrs. Balliet sent us with lunch buckets. We'll be eating lunch in the schoolyard then we'll go in for more lessons before it's time to head home."

"We should bring Benny with us," Jim reasoned. "He's gonna be lonely all by himself with just Mrs. Balliet."

"Benny's not even four years old yet, Jim," May explained. "He's not ready to go to school. But don't worry about him. He'll be just fine, and happy to see us when we get back home."

This seemed to satisfy young Jim and he took off running as the schoolyard came into sight.

Henry Fenner, or Hen as he was commonly called, ran a strict classroom for the children of lower Saylorsburg. He taught all the grades from first through eighth and tolerated no infractions from the students. Although they didn't know it, he always made a point to use a student as an example on the very first day of school in order to make it clear to everyone that he was in charge. Little did Jim know, but he was to be that example today. As Hen Fenner called the class to order, all the students grappled for a seat. Being the youngest student, Jim was unfamiliar with this routine and was slow to act. When he finally realized that he was one of the few not yet seated, he searched out his brother Oliver and went to sit next to him.

"You're in my seat," Jim addressed another boy who was now sitting next to Oliver Jr. "That's my brother. I'm sittin' next to him."

"Yeah, right," the older boy replied as he turned his back to Jim.

Not knowing what to do, and feeling a bit panicked, Jim started pulling on the boy's shirt to pull him out of his seat.

"Get lost, punk!" the boy spat in Jim's direction.

Losing his temper, Jim smacked the boy against his head in an effort to convince him to move. Unfortunately at just that moment, Hen Fenner looked in Jim's direction and singled him out. Pulling Jim to the front of the classroom, the teacher banged on his desk to get the class's attention.

"Now here's a lesson for all of you, and I suggest you learn it quickly. This boy seems to think he can start a fight in my schoolhouse," Hen Fenner warned the class. "Get out in that schoolyard young man, and cut down a switch. Then bring it in to me immediately."

Jim did as he was told, cutting a switch and bringing it right back to his teacher.

"Now this is what will happen to any of you who decide to misbehave during school time," Hen Fenner announced in his most stern voice. He took the switch and whipped Jim on his bare legs to teach him, and all his classmates, a lesson to remember.

Jim took the whipping as best he could, deciding then and there to do nothing again that would bring the attention of the teacher his way. He was a model student for the remainder of the day, fearful to do anything that would result in another whipping.

* * * *

By the middle of October, the Balliets, along with the Nordmark children in their charge, had packed up their things and prepared to head back to their brick house in Saylorsburg for the winter months. Oliver had visited his children once while they were at the farm and convinced himself that they were safe and being cared for. He planned to visit them again when they were back in Saylorsburg for the winter. Once they were moved back, the children were enrolled in the Flyte School, and no one could have been happier than six-year-old Jim. He didn't care if he never saw mean old Hen Fenner again as long as he lived.

The Flyte School was also a one room school house with a wood burning potbelly stove in the center of the room for heating. There was a well outside that supplied drinking water for the students. The teacher would fill a milk pail with water at the start of each day and bring it into the school where it sat on a table near the side door. A dipper hung from a nail next to the table, and the students could take turns drinking from it when they were thirsty. There were outside bathrooms, known as outhouses; one for boys and one for girls.

The children's teacher at the Flyte School was Mr. Pete Faulstick. Although he ran a tight ship, he was a caring man who tried to inspire his students to achieve their highest potential. He often would have to go and fetch Bud, Oliver Jr., and Jim from the barn at the top of the hill where they would stop to play on their walk to school. There were large mounds of hay in the barn and the boys took delight in jumping from the platforms on the sides of the barn into the soft hay. When the boys heard their teacher calling their names as he got closer and closer to the barn, they knew it was time to get going and they would run down the other side of the hill to try and beat Mr. Faulstick back to the schoolhouse.

One day shortly before the Christmas break, Pete Faulstick's patience with his students was put to the ultimate test.

The Flyte School: 1st Row from left: Oliver Jr., 3rd - Bud, Last.
2nd Row From left: Jim, First - Margaret, 6th . 3rd Row From left: May, 6th

"Can I go to the outhouse?" asked Bud Nordmark as he raised his hand during math class.

Mr. Faulstick turned from the front of the class and reluctantly gave Bud permission to go outside.

"Me too?" called out Oliver Jr. as he glanced towards his big brother with a grin. He squirmed in his seat as he looked at Mr. Faulstick with a pleading look. "I gotta go bad!"

"Oh, alright. But hurry back here," replied the exasperated teacher.

Oliver jumped from his seat and headed for the door. When Mr. Faulstick's back was turned again, Jim Nordmark saw his chance and broke for the door as well. Little did Pete Faulstick know, but these brothers were up to their tricks again. As he tried to get back to his math lesson, the relative quiet of his classroom was shaken by the sounds of gunfire.

"Bang, Bang, Bang!"

Everyone ran for the door with Pete Faulstick in the lead. "Take your seats!" he shouted as he ran out the door.

The students did not obey but instead crowded around the door and windows to try and see just what was going on. As Pete Faulstick rounded the corner of the building, headed towards the outhouses, he saw immediately just what was up. Jim and Oliver Jr. were looking up to the roof of the outhouses where Bud Nordmark had climbed with two large rocks. Just as Bud dropped one rock onto the other, Mr. Faulstick found his voice.

"Bud! What the heck…?" he shouted.

But before he could utter another word, the rocks made contact and another loud 'Bang' could be heard throughout the valley. Bud looked over at his teacher with a guilty grin on his face. He quickly shoved whatever was in his hand deep into his pocket and climbed down from the outhouse.

"Give me what's in your pockets!" Mr. Faulstick demanded.

Reluctantly, Bud pulled the .22 shells from his pocket and handed them over to his teacher, knowing full well he was in for big trouble this time. Jim, on the other hand, had no idea that trouble was at hand.

"It's gun shells!" he explained with excitement. "He took 'em from Mr. Balliet's gun case. It's like fireworks!" He could hardly contain himself as he jumped up and down. "He's got more, come on, let's bang 'em!"

Mr. Faulstick was not amused. "Get back in that classroom. And Bud, you'll be staying after class for the rest of the week. Now get back to your math lesson, all of you! If I ever catch you with gun shells in school again, there won't be any school for you!"

As the boys and their teacher turned to go back in the school, all the other students quickly dashed to their seats pretending to be deep in thought, pencils in hand. When recess time came, they were all congratulating Bud on his stunt, thrilled that he had gotten the best of old Pete Faulstick!

* * * *

There were no more behavior problems at the Flyte School that week and soon it was time for the Christmas break. With just two days until Christmas Eve, the Nordmark children were very excited, especially young Benny and Jim. Christmas Eve found them gazing out their bedroom window as they scanned the star filled sky for a glimpse of Santa's sleigh.

"Look!" shouted Benny as he pointed up towards the moon. "I see it! I see it! It's Santa's reindeers!"

"Where?" Jim replied, anxious to see it too. "By the moon?"

"Right under the moon," Benny shouted. "Right there, see it movin'? It's the sleigh!" He quickly turned and flopped on the bed, hiding his face in the pillow. "Don't let him see you, he might not come if he sees you lookin'!"

"I think you're right," Jim answered, wishing it to be true. "It *is* Santa's sleigh. But he's still far away so I don't think he saw us lookin'!" He snuggled down into the bed with Benny as the two giggled with excitement, trying to get to sleep before Santa's arrival.

With morning's light, all the children rushed to the living room to find that Santa had indeed visited during the night. There was an identical present for each one of them. As they tore the paper from the package, they each found a new washcloth, towel, and bar of sweet smelling soap. Although it wasn't the toys they had hoped for, they marveled still at the magic of the nighttime visit from the North Pole.

* * * *

Another year passed and by the spring of 1934, five-year-old Benny, still too young for school, would try to find ways to amuse himself as he waited each day for his brothers and sisters to come back home. One of his favorite pastimes was playing "car" out behind the Balliets' garage. He put together some old boards and a steering wheel and pretended to ride along, making lots of car noises with his mouth.

As the first signs of spring began to appear, Benny decided to make some mud pies. Having watched Eva Balliet cooking and baking, he was pretty sure he knew how it was done. He ran into the chicken house when Mrs. Balliet wasn't looking and shoved two eggs into his pockets. Hiding behind the garage, he happily mixed the eggs with a pile of dirt making a muddy mess. He slapped his hands in the mud, forming the pies and lining them up for baking in his pretend oven. Then he mashed them all together and started over again, enjoying his game for nearly an hour. Finally, he heard the calls of Eva Balliet from the back door.

"Benny!" she shouted impatiently. "Where are

you?"

Not wanting to have her find his mud pies, for which he surely would be punished, Benny jumped up and ran to the house.

"Where have you been?" questioned an angry Mrs. Balliet. "I've been looking for you all over this house. You're not to go outside without my permission and you know it," she scolded as she reached out and slapped him across the face.

It was not her intention, but her fingernails caught the young boy's skin and scratched thin blood lines across his right cheek. "Get in the house!" she said as she pulled Benny in through the door.

That night at the supper table, a worn-out Mrs. Balliet's patience was tested again. As the children all took their place at the table, and grace was said, little Benny looked across the table at the meager offerings.

"Is this all we're having?" the young boy questioned innocently.

Mrs. Balliet had had enough. She backhanded Benny and knocked him off his stool. Fourteen-year-old May came to his defense, only to find herself being sent to her room with no supper at all. The other children all sat quietly as they ate their meal, not wishing to cause any more trouble.

As May lay quietly thinking in her bed that night, she mentally devised a way to escape, and save her brothers and sister from the mistreatment that was becoming more and more commonplace at the Balliets' home. By morning, she was ready to put her plan into action. As she dressed for school, she waited for Margaret to leave the bedroom they shared. May then put a second layer of clothing over her first, waiting until it was almost time to leave for school before going downstairs.

"You barely have time for breakfast," Mrs. Balliet scolded May as she walked through the kitchen.

"I'm not hungry," May replied as she glanced in Mrs. Balliet's direction before quickly heading out the back door.

"Suit yourself," Mrs. Balliet called after her.

* * * *

When the school bell rang at the end of the day, May was nervous and a little scared, but was resolved to put an end to her family's time with the Balliets.

"You go on ahead," she called to her siblings. "I have to stay after school for a bit but I'll be along shortly."

The other children headed off for the trek back home. As soon as they were out of sight, May took off in the opposite direction. It would be a long walk from Saylorsburg to Stroudsburg but maybe she could hitch a ride with someone for at least part of the way.

"Where is your sister?" a disgruntled Eva

Balliet asked when the children returned home without May.

"She had to stay after school for something. She'll be along later," Margaret answered as she repeated May's excuse.

Eva Balliet thought little about May until dinner time arrived and May still had not returned. After dinner she expressed her concern to her husband Oscar.

"I'd better go and tell the sheriff," he reasoned. "If I don't go right away, they may find a way to blame us for that girl's ungrateful behavior. They'll find her and bring her back in no time I'm sure. How far could she have gone?" As he grabbed his jacket and headed out the door, he mumbled under his breath. "Geez, these kids are a lot of work. We never had half this trouble raisin' our own child."

* * * *

An hour after she had left school, with still many miles to walk to reach the Children's Aid Society office, May heard a car horn behind her. As the car pulled over, May could see that it was Mr. Faulstick. He offered her a ride which May was happy to accept.

"Where are you headed, May?" the teacher questioned. "You're a bit far from home, aren't you?"

May had to think quickly. "Oh, I walk into

town quite a bit for Mrs. Balliet. She wants me to take a message to Miss Martin at the Children's Aid."

"Well I can take you the rest of the way," Pete Faulstick smiled in reply as he wondered what May was *really* up to. He couldn't imagine that the Balliets would allow May to walk the nearly ten miles from Saylorsburg to Stroudsburg. Surely something else must be going on here, he reasoned.

*   *   *   *

Just as Oscar Balliet was about to get into his car to drive to the Sheriff's office, Officer Garner pulled his car into the drive.

"Looks like that oldest girl you got livin' here made her way into town, Oscar," Officer Garner explained as he walked towards Mr. Balliet. "They're keepin' her overnight at the Children's Aid. She'll be brought back tomorrow."

"I appreciate you driving out to tell us," Oscar Balliet thanked the officer. "I can't imagine what got into that girl, but I'm sure we'll get it straightened out tomorrow."

"Yeah, well kids can sure get some crazy things in their heads these days," Officer Garner said, shaking his head. "Just didn't want you worryin' about where she was. I'll be seein' ya, Oscar."

*   *   *   *

Miss Martin, with the runaway May in tow, arrived at the Balliet home the following afternoon to try and sort out what had happened. May had already told her about the dinner incident and had also told her in no uncertain terms that if they made her go back there to live, she would just run away again.

Sitting in the living room with the Balliets and the Nordmark children, Miss Martin listened to Mrs. Balliet's side of the story, then glanced in Benny's direction. The first thing she noticed was his scratched cheek.

"What happened to you, Benny?" she inquired of the child.

Before he could speak, Mrs. Balliet interrupted, answering for him. "Oh he just got scratched by the neighbor's cat out in the yard yesterday. He's fine," she explained as she glared at the child, daring him to contradict her.

Benny just sat on his hands, lips sealed.

"Well," Miss Martin concluded the meeting as she knowingly looked in Benny's direction. "May, if you'll come outside with me I'd like to have a word with you in private." She stood and said her good-byes to the Balliets and the children, then stepped outside with May.

"No doubt she's putting the fear of God in that child for running away from a good home," Mrs. Balliet said to her husband. She could not imagine that Miss Martin would believe a fourteen-year-old's story over hers – even if it *was* true. She put the matter out of her mind and went about her day.

* * * *

Imagine Eva Balliet's surprise the next day when Miss Martin again pulled into the driveway, this time with paperwork in her hand.

"Good morning, Mrs. Balliet," began a determined Miss Martin as she stood on the front porch. "I've come with the necessary paperwork to remove the children from your care. If you'll go and gather their things, I'll take Benny now and then collect the other children from school this afternoon."

Eva Balliet opened her mouth to object, but realized there was no changing the situation. Besides, she thought to herself, she really was tired of caring for so many children. They were a lot more work than she had imagined and at her age, she really wasn't up to it. Rather than put up an argument, she turned to gathered the children's belongings and delivered them, along with five-year-old Benny, to the arms of Miss Martin.

"Now maybe there'll be some peace in this house again," were Mrs. Balliet's parting words as she turned her back and slammed the door behind her.

CHAPTER EIGHT

The Kobers & The Kemmerers

Miss Martin collected the five older Nordmark children from the Flyte School later that afternoon, explaining to them that their living situation was about to change.

"May, you and Margaret will be going to live with Mr. and Mrs. Kemmerer in South Stroudsburg. They are a wonderful, Christian couple who are looking forward to having you both come and live with them," Miss Martin said with an upbeat voice.

"What about our brothers?" May asked with worry. "Where are our brothers going to live?"

"Well boys," Miss Martin smiled in Bud's direction. "You will be pleased to know that you're headed to the Kober family. They live on a farm in Shawnee that borders the Delaware River. Mr. and Mrs. Kober even have a son not much older than you, Bud. His name is Frankie and I'm sure you'll all get along just fine."

"I'm sure we'll do *just* fine," mused Bud as he contemplated to himself just what sort of mischief he might be able to conjure up on the Kobers' farm.

"What about school?" Oliver Jr. asked quietly. "Do we still get to go to the Flyte School?"

Back: Frankie Kober, May, Bud, Oliver, Jr.
Front: Jim, Margaret, Benny

"Oh I'm afraid not," replied Miss Martin. "That would be much too far. Your new school will be the Smithfield Elementary School."

Oliver Jr. slid down in his seat, covering his face with his hands. He liked going to the Flyte School and he was going to miss spending the summer at the Balliets' farm in Cherry Valley. He wished things would stop changing all the time and he worried about what kind of family the Kobers would be. If only his dad would come and get them, he wished silently. As if she could read his mind, his sister May broke the silence.

"Where is our father, Miss Martin?" she found the courage to ask. "Why hasn't he come to get us yet?"

Miss Martin understood the children's anguish. She had seen it time and time again with the children in her care. "From what I understand, May, your father is still trying to find steady work and a place for all of you to live. It's very hard for folks, with the country in such a depression. Why, just the other day I read in the newspaper that one in every five workers is out of a job. That comes to over twelve million people in the whole country. Things are very bad, and I'm sure your dad's trying the best he can. He has visited you at the Balliets, right?"

"Yes, he's been to see us. And he came to school once to see us too, but he didn't tell us when he's coming back for us," May replied with defeat. "I'm sure the Kemmerers and the Kobers will be much better for us than the Balliets' house until he can come and get us." May folded her arms across her chest and leaned her head against the window of Miss Martin's car, as she considered what might lie ahead.

* * * *

Jesse and Frank Kober welcomed the four Nordmark brothers into their home, and the three oldest boys began attending school with Frankie Jr.

Mrs. Kober was a warm and cheerful lady and Benny quickly settled into his new routine of tagging along behind her during the day or playing with some of Frankie's old toy cars while he waited for his brothers to return each afternoon. Frankie had an entire collection of small toy cars, as well as little Sonoco gas stations with pumps and signs. Benny could lie on the floor playing with them for hours as he made believe that he was driving the cars up and over the floorboards, stopping in for gas, and filling the tires with air.

Frank Kober was a tall, stern, intimidating looking man who had very little to say. He not only worked his farm in Shawnee, but he also had a job in East Stroudsburg.

Bud, Oliver Jr., Jim and Benny quickly made friends with Frankie and with summer on the horizon, the five boys found all sorts of fun things to do. There was a Boy Scout Camp on the banks of the Delaware River just about a mile from the

Kobers' farm and the boys would frequently go there in the evenings to watch movies. They spent long summer afternoons swimming in the river and lying in the sun. One day Bud decided that it was time for little Benny to learn how to swim.

"Come on Benny," he coaxed his brother closer to the water's edge. "You'll be old enough to go to school come September, so I'd say you're old enough to learn how to swim." When Benny was ankle deep, Bud grabbed him and with a laugh, tossed him out into the river just above his head.

Little Benny came up spitting and sputtering while Bud gave him his first swimming lesson.

"Put your hands in front of you like this," Bud demonstrated in doggie paddle fashion. "Pull the water with each hand and kick your feet!"

A frightened Benny kicked like mad and paddled his hands as he leaned his head up and back trying to keep his nose above water. The other boys laughed and giggled at his effort. Just as he was nearing shore, Bud picked him up and tossed him back out again. By the third toss, Benny was doggie paddling all around and feeling quite proud of his accomplishment!

* * * *

Of course there was work to do on the Kobers' farm too. Many a day was spent in the field pulling mustard weeds while the heat of the noonday sun baked the earth. The Kobers' farmhouse used carbolite for lighting. The boys had never seen anything other than kerosene used for lighting and Jim was fascinated as he helped Frank Kober pour lime into the underground tank which created a gas. The gas then traveled through a pipe running into the house and up the walls into each room where the gas would power a chandelier.

"These Kobers must really be rich," Jim marveled to himself. "Automatic gas and chandeliers too!" He found himself hoping that they could stay with the Kobers forever.

One Sunday afternoon after the boys had been with the Kobers for several months, they had a surprise visit from their sisters.

"Look who's coming to visit!" Mrs. Kober called to the boys as they finished their milking in the barn.

An old four-door car was coming up the road and headed for the barn. As soon as it stopped, out jumped May and Margaret, anxious to see their brothers. After happy shouts of greeting and plenty of hugs, Mrs. Kober left the children alone to spend some time together.

"So how's it going here?" May asked her brothers cautiously.

"Oh we're doing just fine," Oliver Jr. said with a smile. "I miss my old school but there's lots of fun things to do here, and we get to go to the river and swim, and that's fun!"

The other boys chimed in with stories of their

own which warmed May's heart as she realized that her brothers were doing okay.

"How about you and Cricket?" Bud finally asked. "How's things goin' where you are?"

"Just fine," smiled May. "And I'm proud to say that I graduated eighth grade with such good marks that they named me salutatorian."

"Salubadorian? What's that?" asked a puzzled Benny.

"Not Salubadorian, silly. Salutatorian. That's a fancy name for second highest grade in the class. And now I'm off to high school in the fall."

The boys congratulated May on her award, although they didn't really understand just what an honor it was.

"So why don't you show us around this place?" May suggested as she took little Benny by the hand and started walking towards the barn.

The six Nordmark children headed off to spend the afternoon together, and the girls stayed for dinner with the Kober family before the Kemmerers came back to pick them up. It was a wonderful surprise visit and they were all sorry to see it come to an end. The Kemmerers promised to bring the girls back again when time allowed, which helped to satisfy the children as they waved good-bye.

Oliver Jr. and Benny Playing in the Snow

CHAPTER NINE

A Happy Reunion

The four Nordmark brothers stayed with the Kober family in Shawnee Valley for nearly two years. By the fall of 1936, they were settled into a familiar routine and although they missed their father and sisters, they knew that they had it much better than some children of the Depression. Newspaper accounts routinely told of long bread lines where people stood for hours just to receive a small ration of food. Work continued to be very scarce and families were being split apart on a regular basis. Organizations like the Children's Aid Society were doing their best to help as many children as they could, but the need was overwhelming.

Oliver, who had been scraping by as best he could while all the time trying to find steady work, finally got the break he needed. One of President Roosevelt's programs to get men back to work was called the Works Progress Administration or WPA for short. Since its inception in 1935, Oliver had kept his name on the list and finally, in the summer of 1936, he was accepted into the program and given work, along with many other men, rebuilding roads in Stroudsburg. Oliver worked hard, although no one in the WPA was allowed to work more than thirty hours a week, and the pay for laborers was a meager eighteen cents an hour. Nevertheless, he saved all the money he possibly could until he had enough to pay rent on a small bungalow. On his first day off, he visited the Children's Aid Society's office.

"Why hello Oliver," smiled Miss Martin as Oliver walked through the door, hat in hand. "Are you here to arrange a visit with the children?"

"No, Miss Martin," Oliver replied. "I'm here to see just what I gotta do to get my kids back."

"Get them back? Has there been a change in your situation?" Miss Martin inquired. She would hate to allow the children to be pulled out of their foster homes only to be quickly disappointed if Oliver wasn't truly ready to care for them again.

"Yes ma'am, there's been a big change, I'm happy to say," Oliver grinned. "I been workin' for the WPA and I saved up enough money to rent a small bungalow out on Route 209, just outside of East Stroudsburg. It's not much, but it's more than some folks got these days."

"That's wonderful news, Oliver!" Miss Martin said genuinely. "I'll need to drive out and inspect it before we can transfer the children there. Jot down the address, and I'll see if I can stop out later today."

Oliver picked up the pencil on Miss Martin's desk and wrote down the address of his new home, then smiled again at Miss Martin as he turned to leave. "I'll be lookin' for you later today then, and

100

thank you Miss Martin, for all you've done to help my family."

* * * *

Miss Martin did indeed visit Oliver that evening when she had finished her work at the office. The bungalow was even smaller than she had imagined and there was no running water or electricity. Rather than flatly deny Oliver his children, she made the decision to allow him to bring the four boys to his new home. There just would not have been any privacy for the young girls, who were now eleven and sixteen years old, and Miss Martin was able to convince Oliver that the girls would be better off staying where they were for the time being.

"I'll visit the Kobers' farm tomorrow and let them know that you're able to take the boys back," Miss Martin said as she shook Oliver's hand. "Then I'll go back on Wednesday evening and bring them here to you."

"I'll be here," Oliver replied. "I'll be here waiting."

* * * *

The Nordmark brothers – Bud who was almost fourteen, Oliver Jr. who was twelve, Jim who would be ten in two months time, and Benny who was now seven-and-a-half – were shocked and excited by the news that Miss Martin brought the following afternoon. They were GOING HOME! They couldn't believe it! The next two days couldn't pass fast enough and when Miss Martin finally came on Wednesday evening, they had said their good-byes to the Kobers and were packed and ready to go.

"Have you forgotten your manners?" Miss Martin asked as she nodded in the direction of Frank and Jesse Kober who stood on the front porch of the farmhouse.

"Thank you! Thank you!" the four boys smiled and called to the Kobers.

"You're very welcome," Mrs. Kober replied with a smile. "Now you boys mind yourselves for your dad, you hear me?"

"We will!" they called back in unison as they climbed into Miss Martin's car and waved their final good-bye.

* * * *

Oliver was anxiously waiting outside the bungalow when Miss Martin pulled up and the boys jumped out, running to greet their father. Then they quickly raced inside to investigate their new home.

"Good luck, Oliver," Miss Martin said. "Be sure and contact us if anything happens that causes your situation to change."

"I'll do that, Miss Martin," Oliver replied. "But

for now, I got my boys back," he smiled.

* * * *

Oliver's sons were thrilled to be back with their dad and quickly learned to overlook the shortcomings of their new home. Because there was no running water, one of the boys' regular chores was to bring water to the house from a nearby spring. The spring water was crystal clear and watercress grew all around the edges. Oliver used kerosene lamps to light the small home at night and all four boys would spend hours trying to make different animal shadows on the wall with their hands. There was an outhouse in the backyard and the children had bowls under the beds in case they needed to relieve themselves during the night. Although the boys had to change schools yet again – from Smithfield Elementary to Clearview Elementary – they didn't mind at all this time since it meant they could be with their father. As fall turned quickly to winter in the Pocono Mountains, the boys discovered the joys of living where there were plenty of hills nearby.

"Let's go and see if some of those kids will let us take a turn on their skis," a hopeful Jim suggested to his brothers as he watched from the window at a group of children who were sledding and skiing on the hill just beyond their house.

It was early on a Saturday morning and the brothers all agreed it was worth a try as they reached for their coats and boots. They raced out the door and headed for the hill.

"Hey Joey!" Benny called to a boy he recognized from school. "Can I take a turn on your sled?"

Joey pulled his sled over to where the Nordmark boys had gathered. "Sure," he said as he offered his sled to his classmate. "I need a rest anyway. It's quick going down, but a lot harder coming up!"

Joey flopped down in the snow as Benny walked with the sled over to the top of the hill. Without even thinking, he jumped on the sled and headed down the hill. As the sled picked up speed, Benny realized that he had no idea how to steer this contraption and his heart began to race. The thrill of the ride, with the wind racing across his face, soon became secondary to the large tree that he realized he was headed straight for.

Benny screamed as he closed his eyes. Within seconds, he had run head long into the tree and was thrown off to one side. Startled and afraid, he lay in the snow and shouted at the top of his lungs, "Help! My neck's broke! I'm dead!"

Bud, who had watched the whole thing, ran down the hill with Oliver Jr. and Jim close behind. He reached Benny in no time, quickly surveyed the situation and began to laugh.

"You're not dead. Get up, ya goof ball!" Bud smiled, as Benny rolled slowly to one side. "You wouldn't be able to roll over if your neck was broke," Bud was quick to point out. "Come on!" he called as he grabbed the sled and headed back up the hill, anxious to take a turn himself.

Benny slowly realized he was, in fact, going to be okay. He struggled back up the hill, deciding he had had just about enough sledding for one day. In the meantime, Oliver Jr. and Jim had reached the top of the hill. As they watched some kids on the hill who had skis, Jim came up with an idea to make their own skis.

"Oliver, come on," he said as he ran towards the bungalow, stopping next to an old barrel. "Help me break this apart," Jim said with excitement. "We can use these barrel staves for skis."

As they worked at breaking the barrel apart, Oliver Jr. realized there was a problem. "How we gonna keep our feet on these staves?"

"Hmm. Well, I guess we gotta tie 'em on somehow," Jim answered as his mind raced to figure it out. "I'll be right back!"

Jim ran into the house and quickly returned with two old leather belt straps, a hammer and a few nails. "This oughta do the job," he mused as he got to work nailing the straps to the staves and then looping them up and tying them around his ankle. "Yep! I think this will work, Oliver. Come on!"

Oliver Jr. grabbed one more stave, the hammer and nails, and headed towards the top of the hill. Jim hobbled behind with the barrel stave tied onto his foot and the second length of leather strap in his hand.

"I'll try it out first," Jim insisted as he took the second stave, hammered the straps to it and tied it to his other foot. "Here I go!" Jim shouted as he leaned forward and took off down the hill. "Whoa!" was the next thing Oliver Jr. heard as Jim crashed onto his bottom with sprays of powdery snow billowing up all around him.

"My turn next!" Oliver Jr. said with excitement. "Come on back, Jim. It's my turn!"

The brothers took turns for the rest of the morning skiing mostly on their bottoms but occasionally staying upright for the better part of the hill. They couldn't remember when they had had so much fun. When their dad finally called them in for lunch, it suddenly dawned on them just how tired, cold and hungry they were. Skiing and sledding sure worked up their appetites!

* * * *

With the spring of 1937 came the chance for an even more exciting adventure – one that Bud, Oliver Jr., Jim, and Benny would remember with a smile for the rest of their lives! It was a sunny Sunday afternoon when Oliver told his boys of a surprise that he had been saving money for, a little each week, until he had enough.

"You know where that Piper's Airport is just over the hill?" Oliver asked his sons with a smile.

"Well today we're gonna go for an airplane ride!"

"An airplane ride?" the boys asked in unison.

"A real airplane?" asked a skeptical Bud.

"Yep, a real airplane," replied Oliver. "Now go and get your shoes on. We're headed over there right now."

Four boys went scurrying around looking for their shoes. Jim quickly realized that *his* shoes were nowhere to be found. Rather than ruin the excitement of the moment with what he considered to be a trivial problem, he reached for an old pair of his father's rubbers, wrapped canning jar rings around them to hold them on, and took off out the door behind his brothers. As the boys followed their dad up and over the hill towards the airport, they could hardly contain their excitement.

"Look at the planes!" shouted Benny. "Which one's gonna be our plane?" he wondered.

"Well, we'll just have to see when we get there," Oliver answered his youngest son as everyone hurried towards the airstrip.

As they approached the Piper Air Field, Oliver introduced himself and his boys to the first man they came upon. They were directed to a small building where Oliver paid for a fifteen-minute ride for all five of them and they waited anxiously to board the plane. As the Ford Tri-Motor airplane came in for a landing, the boys were jumping up and down with anticipation. As it came to a stop and the door opened, the boys took off like a shot, with Jim at the rear running along merrily in his flapping rubbers. As soon as the previous passengers climbed out of the plane, the boys jumped aboard. Since this was a four passenger plane, the boys had to share seats and Benny climbed up on his dad's lap next to the window.

As soon as everyone was seated the pilot closed the door, climbed into his seat, and began taxiing down the grassy runway. The small plane was filled with the cries of "oohs!" and "aahs!" as it picked up speed and gently lifted off the ground headed skyward.

Benny looked out the window and caught sight of the landing wheels gliding up and down on the struts and all of a sudden he began to cry.

"What's wrong Benny?" Oliver asked his son.

"Look!" he pointed out the window. "We're gonna lose our wheels, we're gonna crash!" his voice quivered through the tears running down his cheeks.

"No, no, we're not going to crash," Oliver tried to console him. "They're supposed to do that."

But little Benny was not convinced and he continued to cry throughout the ride. The other boys were delighted by the sensation of flying high above the ground. They chattered nonstop throughout their short ride and Oliver was pleased that he could bring such joy to their faces after everything they had been through. He silently assured himself that it was worth every penny.

When the plane landed safely, much to Benny's surprise, the boys reluctantly climbed out.

"Can we go up again?" Benny asked with renewed excitement now that he knew the plane wouldn't crash. "Can we, can we?"

"No, just one ride per family," Oliver smiled. "It's another family's turn now."

The boys and Oliver headed back to the bungalow full of talk about their exciting adventure, eager to share the story with their friends once they got back to school.

Francis (Bud) Nordmark

CHAPTER TEN

Brushy Mountain

As the summer of 1937 approached, Oliver had the opportunity to move his boys to a larger home off of Route 447 in Analomink. It was an area called Brushy Mountain and the large stone house, although in great need of repair, would give the boys a lot more space. It was located at the end of a 500 ft. long gravel drive with woods on either side. There was only one neighbor, the Widmer family, whose house was about 200 feet off to one side of Oliver's newly rented house. The roof leaked, so Oliver placed many basins and buckets around the attic to catch the water before it could reach the living spaces below. There was no electric and no running water but there was a well in the yard with a bucket tied to a rope where they could draw fresh water. The house was heated with a large coal burning furnace in the basement. The heat would rise up through the large grate in the floor and keep the entire house nice and warm once winter came around again. For bathing, Oliver would fill a large tub in the kitchen with heated water from the stove and each boy would take his turn getting clean. After the family had lived on Brushy Mountain for a short time, Oliver had the opportunity to meet his neighbor who shared some very advantageous information.

"Name's Oliver Nordmark," Oliver said as he extended his hand to the man as the two met between the properties one summer evening.

"Joe Widmer," smiled Oliver's neighbor. "I seen you got some boys, Oliver. I got four sons myself and one daughter."

"Yep, I got four sons too."

"I notice you got no lights in the house at night. No electric?" questioned Joe.

"No, there's no electric, but I got some kerosene lamps," replied Oliver who was used to having no electric.

"Well, I'll tell you what to do if you want electric," Joe smiled slyly. "You just have to climb up that pole and hook ya up a line to the rooftop connection over there and you'll have electric free of charge." Joe motioned from the pole to the top of Oliver's house.

"Is that what you did?" Oliver asked his neighbor.

"Well, no, we got electric service with our rent, but I got no qualms tellin' you how to get it for free. Hey, every man for himself is what I say in these hard times."

Oliver thanked his neighbor for the suggestion and walked back to his house pondering the idea. He was in great shape from all the hard work he did, so climbing the utility pole would be no trouble, and they certainly could benefit from having electricity in the house. By the next day,

Oliver had decided to give it a try – nothing ventured, nothing gained, that's what Oliver remembered his own father saying. Oliver, too, had been living by that motto for most of his life. He climbed the pole and made the connection with the help of Bud who waited on the roof of the house holding the wire. With the wires connected, and the purchase of two used lamps from the Salvation Army Thrift Store, the Nordmarks had electric for the first time!

* * * *

With the end of the school year came a newfound freedom for the boys. Since Oliver would still need to go to work with the WPA, his plan was to leave the boys alone during the day. He reasoned that since Bud was nearly fifteen, he could oversee any problems that might come up. After all, Oliver himself had been on his own since he was fifteen so it didn't seem like a problem in his mind. Since Oliver had spent his childhood working hard on farms in Kansas, he wanted things to be different for his sons. He was very lenient, letting them explore the world around Brushy Mountain to their hearts content. He never punished them for their antics – he rarely even corrected them. Boys will be boys, he figured, and his boys could do no wrong in Oliver's eyes.

The first place that the boys discovered as they ventured from the stone house was Stokes' Mill on

Broadhead's Creek. On hot sunny days they would walk down the hill, cross the cinder bed railroad tracks in their bare feet and spend the day swimming and sunning on the large rocks that bordered the creek. There was a waterfall that, over time, had carved many narrow, shallow streams in the rock formations below. Bud quickly became skilled at catching trout by wading up the stream, his hands feeling under the water along the crevices of rock until he found a fish. In one smooth motion, he would flip the fish out of the water and onto the smooth flat rocks. Further down the creek, the streams merged into a crystal clear body of water that was seventy-five feet wide and anywhere from two to eight feet deep. This is where all the local children would gather to swim. The boys would stay there all day, bringing raisins and candy bars to eat for lunch. It was so much fun, they wished that summer could go on forever!

* * * *

When they weren't swimming, Bud, Oliver Jr., Jim, and Benny found lots of other ways to amuse themselves during those long summer days. Bud, who had become quite the marksman, enjoyed impressing his younger brothers with his skill. One day, he decided to include them in his hobby.

"Hey, Oliver!" he called to his brother. "Let me show you what I can do."

Oliver came running, with Jim and Benny just

behind him, eager to see what skill Bud had perfected this time.

"Here, take this stick and put it in your mouth," Bud instructed his willing brother. "Now turn sideways and don't move."

Oliver Jr. did as he was told and Bud stepped back about twenty feet. Suddenly, and without warning, there was a loud pop from Bud's .22 rifle and the stick was blown out of Oliver's mouth.

"Wow!" shouted Jim and Benny in unison. "Do it again, do it again!"

Oliver Jr. was stunned as he reached down for the stick. "You tryin' to kill me or something?" he yelled at Bud.

"Do it again, Oliver!" Jim begged his brother.

"No way, Jim. *You* can do it, not me!"

"Here ya go, Jim," Bud coaxed his younger brother. "You can have a turn, only you can do it better than Oliver. Here, put this cigarette in your mouth," Bud said as he pulled one of his father's hand rolled cigarettes from his pocket and handed it to Jim.

Sticking the cigarette in his mouth, Jim turned sideways giggling.

"Now I'll show you my *superior* shooting skills," Bud announced as he backed up another twenty feet. "Just don't move Jim," he casually instructed. With that, the boys heard the telltale loud pop from the rifle as the cigarette disintegrated into tiny shreds and fell to the ground.

"My turn, my turn!" an excited Benny shouted.

"Naw, you're too young for a cigarette," Bud chided the eight-year-old. "Here, take this and put it on your head," he said as he walked to the side of the house and picked up an old rusty tin can.

"On my head?" a now worried Benny asked. "Not on my head!"

"Alright, then hold it out to the side like this," Bud demonstrated.

Benny did as he was told, while Bud backed up yet another ten feet. He took aim and fired, striking the can dead on.

"Ouch! You hit me!" Benny called as tears came to his eyes. "The bullet hit my face!" he cried as he clutched his cheek.

Bud, who knew he had hit only the can, came running up to check on his little brother. As he pried Benny's hand away from his cheek, he saw a bright red patch. Glancing towards the ground, Bud saw the rim of the can and put two and two together.

"You're alright, Benny," he consoled his brother. "Look, the bullet must've nicked the rim of the can and a little sliver of metal just stung you in the face, that's all. I didn't hit you, you'll be fine."

"I'm tellin' Dad when he gets home!" Benny cried, still clutching his cheek.

"Now don't go and do a thing like that," Bud persuaded him. "I'll tell you what. I'll teach you to shoot the gun yourself if ya keep this between us and don't be tellin' Dad. What do ya say?"

The boys all agreed to stay quiet about the incident, and Bud spent the rest of the afternoon letting his brothers take turns shooting the .22 rifle. They had so much fun, they quickly forgot about the near miss.

* * * *

Thanks to Bud's introduction and continued encouragement, all of the boys became very adept at shooting their father's gun. Eventually, after they were all comfortable handling the rife, they showed their father how they could hit a target on a faraway tree. Oliver was proud of his sons' marksmanship skills, thinking very little about any danger that might be involved. He soon taught them how to control the rat population in the basement by placing bits of food at the bottom of the cellar steps. When a rat would come to eat the food, Oliver, who was sitting at the top of the stairs, would casually pick up the .22 rifle from his lap and shoot the rat as it ate. The boys got quite a kick out of this and soon took over the pest control needs in the house.

With B.B. guns that Oliver had bought for the boys from a second hand sale, the boys devised a game of crouching behind the sofa, taking aim at the cuckoo clock above the fireplace. When the bird popped out of its little door, a single shot would knock off a wing, or part of it's beak until eventually there was very little left that resembled a bird at all.

One day, Benny was home alone when two classmates approached the house. Stu Pifer and Bill Widmer had gotten into an argument with Benny at school and they had come to settle a score. They went from door to door and from window to window trying to break into the house to exact their revenge. Panicked, Benny looked around for a way to defend himself when he laid eyes on the rifle. He picked it up, chambered a round and walked towards a window. He opened the window just far enough to stick the rifle out as he shouted to the boys.

"Get away from our house!" Benny called out.

Bill and Stu rounded the corner expecting to grab Benny but quickly saw the gun sticking out the window and took off running down the long driveway.

Benny decided it was the perfect time to teach these two a lesson. He aimed at the nearby pigeon coop and fired off a round just to give the bullies a scare.

"I'm hit! I'm hit!" shouted a terrified Stu Pifer as he threw his hands into the air, ducking behind a tree.

Benny laughed so hard he fell to the floor. He really showed those two! When he got back up and peeked out the window, Bill and Stu were long gone and Benny figured that would be the end of that.

When Oliver came home from work that afternoon, he was stopped as he turned into the driveway by Stu Pifer's father, John.

"Looks like you got a hellion you're raisin' up there in that house," began John as Oliver stepped from his car.

"What do ya mean?" Oliver questioned.

"That boy of yours tried to kill my Stu today. Shot right at him from the window," John shared. "Lucky thing for him he ain't much of a shot, seein' as he missed him. I got half a mind to call the sheriff and see what he's got to say about this."

"Now, don't be doin' that," Oliver cautioned. "We don't want the law up here lookin' things over too closely now do we?"

John knew Oliver had a good point. It was best to settle these things among neighbors. With the times being what they were, there was plenty of minor law breaking going on just to get by. No sense in bringing the law around, stickin' their nose into things.

"Well, as long as you're tellin' me you're gonna handle it, I'll be leavin' it up to you," John decided. "And keep those guns away from those boys while you're at work!"

John turned and headed towards his house as Oliver climbed back into his old car and headed up the drive. Benny and Jim met Oliver's car about half way up the driveway and jumped onto the running boards to ride the rest of the way up to the house.

"Did ya bring us anything?" they shouted in unison.

"Well, I did bring ya somethin'," Oliver said as he pulled a box from the back of the car. He had stopped at the Salvation Army store on his way home and brought some warmer clothes for the coming fall weather. The boys quickly dug into it to see what they could find.

"Hey, I'll take this!" Benny smiled as he pulled out a heavy red sweater and held it up.

"Alright, let's take this stuff in the house," Oliver told the boys. "And Benny I want to talk to you when we get inside."

Once inside the house, Oliver told Benny about his encounter with Stu Pifer's father.

"Aw, Dad," Benny began in his defense. "I was just scarin' him. If I wanted to hit him, he'd be dead. I shot at the pigeon coop and he started screamin' that he was hit. They came up here tryin' to beat me up cause we had a fight in school. But I showed them," Benny concluded his story proudly.

"Look, Benny," Oliver began in explanation. "I know you were just defendin' yourself but you can't be shootin' at kids, even if you're aimin' at the pigeon coop. If someone is pickin' on you, throw stones at 'em. Or better yet, hit 'em with a big stick. You're not big enough to kill 'em, but you could really hurt 'em. That'll teach 'em to stay clear of you." Having given his best fatherly advice, Oliver considered the matter closed and went to make a pot of macaroni for dinner.

* * * *

Summers on Brushy Mountain were full of fun for the Nordmark boys. Oliver planted a large garden each summer full of lettuce and tomatoes that the boys used for making sandwiches. They built wooden cages and captured small woodland critters that they kept on the front porch. They made a game of lowering Benny down into the deep well as he clung to the bucket and they swung from vines that hung in the woods pretending to be Tarzan. They laid corn silk on the roof of the house to dry, then rolled it into cigarettes for themselves. On sunny days, one of their most ambitious adventures involved removing the large heavy mirror from the living room wall and carrying it to the top of a sloping shale pit about three hundred yards from the house. It would take at least two boys to hold the mirror in such a way that it would catch the sun's reflection and shine it onto the windshields of unsuspecting cars as they drove down Route 447. When they tired of trying to cause car crashes, the boys would take turns shooting at the large boulders that lined the bottom of the pit just to hear the whine of the ricochet when one of them scored a hit. It was a carefree life, and they were all disappointed when summer would come to an end, signaling the return to school and a more structured, supervised schedule.

Jim & Oliver, Jr. at the 6th Street Apartment

CHAPTER ELEVEN

Moving On

The winter of 1938 brought subtle changes to life on Brushy Mountain that foretold of even harder times to come. Food became more and more scarce with sometimes only a pot of noodles on the stove to last for several days. One day as the boys watched through the window for their father to arrive home, they noticed the neighbor's chickens pecking at the ground.

"Sure would be nice to have chicken for dinner sometimes," Oliver Jr. mused aloud.

"Let's shoot one of their chickens," suggested Jim.

"Naw, we can't shoot 'em. Someone's likely to hear the shot and come over here to investigate," reasoned Bud. "But that doesn't mean we can't have a chicken dinner. Come on with me," he led his brothers.

Once outside, Bud took command. Leaving his brothers at the property line, he snuck over to the Widmers' grain bucket and scooped up a handful of chicken feed, then ran back before being seen.

"Now here's what we do," Bud began. "Toss bits of chicken feed over towards the chickens. As soon as we get one's attention, we'll toss the feed a little closer and then a little closer until we lead a chicken all the way into the basement."

All the boys tossed small bits of feed towards the chickens and quickly they had the attention of one large hen. Their plan worked and once they had the hen in the cellar, they slammed the doors shut.

"Wait till Dad sees we caught a chicken for dinner!" Benny smiled.

When Oliver arrived home, the boys were anxious to lead him down the cellar stairs to proudly show him the hen. When they explained how they had captured the chicken, Oliver was concerned, but impressed as well.

"Well, I don't think you should be doin' that again. But as long as it's here, we'd better eat it right away before anyone notices it's missing. Bud you go and put a pot of water on the stove while I get it ready for cookin'. You other boys go on upstairs."

"But we wanna watch!" Jim complained. "Are ya gonna shoot it or chop it's head off?"

Oliver smiled and shook his head. "No I'm not gonna shoot it or chop its head off. I'm just gonna break its neck and pluck the feather off. Now get upstairs," he said as he shooed the three younger boys up to the kitchen.

The meal in the Nordmark's house was delicious that night as each boy swore a vow of secrecy as to the fate of the fat hen.

* * * *

Oliver soon ran out of money to purchase coal to heat the house, so he and his two oldest sons took on the common practice during the Depression of "picking coal". The railroad yard, with multiple tracks, was only about a mile from their house. On winter evenings, there would sometimes be coal cars full of coal parked on the tracks. Oliver would drive his car as close to the tracks as possible, and the boys would fill burlap bags with as much coal as they could grab. Oliver reasoned to the boys that this was not the same as stealing because when the trains traveled along the tracks, plenty of coal would typically spill off the top of each coal car landing on either side of the tracks. Picking up spilled coal off the ground was perfectly legal so this was really the same thing, only they were picking it before it fell. Either way, it was spare coal and they could certainly put it to good use heating their house.

Since there wasn't always enough food, the boys sometimes went to school without a lunch, claiming that they had just forgotten to bring one. When they did have a lunch, it usually was just peanut butter on bread, but they never complained. One day, while opening his meager peanut butter lunch, Benny looked across his desk and eyed his classmate, Glenn Coster, as he was opening his lunch pail. Glenn's family was in a much better financial situation than most families in the area and although he'd never been there, Benny had heard that they lived in a big fancy house and even had servants.

"Whatcha got there?" an eager Benny asked the boy.

"Cupcakes," replied Glenn as if it were the most common of things to bring in one's lunch pail.

Benny, who never had the pleasure of such treats, could not take his eyes off the confections. There were two cupcakes, each heaped high with dark green icing. He could just taste the sweetness of that icing as his tongue involuntarily came out of his mouth and brushed along the edge of his top lip. He knew he *had* to have one.

"Hey Glenn," Benny began his ploy. "I've got a peanut butter sandwich here that I'll trade you for one of your cupcakes."

Glenn glanced over at Benny, rolled his eyes and returned his attention to his lunch.

"It's really creamy. In fact, there's probably enough peanut butter here to make two sandwiches, that's how good it is," Benny tried his best to convince his classmate. "I'll tell you what. I'm so nice, I'll trade you the whole sandwich for *half* a cupcake." That oughta do it, he reasoned as he sat back, folding his arms across his chest.

Glenn was not impressed. "Benny, if you think I'm gonna give one of these fancy cupcakes to a cunnerman from Brushy Mountain, you must be dumber than you look. I don't even like peanut butter, and no one's eatin' these cupcakes but me," Glenn said with finality as he sank his teeth deep into the first cupcake.

Benny, feeling defeated, turned his back and began eating his sandwich, secretly vowing to himself that *one day,* he would have all the cupcakes he wanted – and candy and ice cream too.

* * * *

Shortly after the incident at school, Benny and his brothers came home to find that Oliver was abruptly moving them out of their house on Brushy Mountain and into a tiny apartment on 6th Street in Stroudsburg. There was no explanation given, but Oliver moved about with a sense of purpose and urgency as he gathered up their few belongings.

"Can we take our critters with us?" Jim asked as he looked towards the front porch where they kept their collection of cages.

"No, just take them back into the woods," Oliver instructed as he continued packing.

Jim and Benny carried the cages, one at a time, to the edge of the woods and ceremoniously released their chipmunk, turtle, snake, and squirrel back into their natural habitats.

Living in town was very different from living on the mountain, beginning with the amount of space they had. Their apartment was on the second floor and consisted of just three rooms. The front room was the living room where there were two sofa beds that transformed the room into the boys' bedroom at night. It was so small that when the beds were opened up, they could easily jump from one bed to the other. Jim and Benny quickly made up a game where Jim would lay on his back, knees pulled tightly against his chest. Benny would sit on his feet and on the count of three, Jim would catapult his younger brother across the room to the older boys' bed. Each safe landing brought cheers and laughter from the young boys. The room had a large potbelly stove with a stovepipe leading to the chimney located in the wall. A bucket of coal sat next to the stove that would get cherry red as it provided heat for the entire apartment. Bud and Oliver Jr. enjoyed tossing .22 caliber shells into the stove just to hear them explode. It was like fireworks inside, they explained to their father who only laughed at their ingenuity.

Just beyond the living room, was a small alcove that provided sleeping space for Oliver. Across from the alcove was the only real bedroom in the apartment. The boys were delighted to find that shortly after they moved in, their sisters May and Margaret joined them, occupying the small bedroom. At the back of the house was a tiny kitchen with an iron, wood burning stove and a small table. A back door opened onto a small porch and wooden stairs, which led down to the back of the building.

* * * *

May, who was now eighteen and about to graduate from high school, was not happy about her move to 6th Street. She and Margaret had been living with the Kemmerers in South Stroudsburg, and were getting along just fine. The Kemmerers had also taken in two brothers, Kenny and Edgar Hall, who were in need of a home. May and Edgar had grown quite fond of one another and often spent time daydreaming about their future, once they were out of school and on their own.

"Look at this." May pointed to her school yearbook as she lay on the bed she shared with Margaret. It was late and Margaret was tired, wishing that May would turn off the light so she could get some sleep. Margaret glanced over to the page where May's senior picture was lined up alongside the other graduates from Stroudsburg High School. "It says, 'Will someday be in the HALL of Fame'."

"What's that supposed to mean?" Margaret asked with little interest. "You think you're gonna be famous or something?"

"No, silly," May replied. "Don't you get it? *Hall* of Fame? As in *Edgar Hall* of fame?"

A smile came to Margaret's face as she realized what the comment was referring to. "Are you going to marry him?" she asked with renewed interest. "Did he ask you to marry him?"

"Well, not yet," May confided. "But I'm sure he was going to, and then we had to move back in here with Father."

"Well, if he's going to ask you to marry him, he can do it whether you're living here or at the Kemmerers," Margaret reasoned. "You're too young to get married yet anyway."

"I most certainly am not," May protested. "Our own mother was not quite sixteen when she married and I'm two years past that. I can get married anytime I choose to."

"Then we'll just have to see if Edgar gets up the nerve and asks you, won't we?" Margaret said as she turned her back to May and pulled the covers closer to her chin.

"He'll ask me," May whispered to herself as she reached up and turned out the light. "He'll ask me."

*　*　*　*

Shortly after the move to 6th Street, Oliver learned of a program that the government had started for young men. It was called the Civilian Conservation Corp, or CCC for short, and it provided work for young men between the ages of seventeen and twenty-three. This program was part of the Unemployment Relief Act and paid the young men thirty dollars a month to dig ditches, fight fires, build reservoirs and other projects. The participants would live in camps operated by the army reserves. Two thirds of the young man's pay would be sent home to his family and Oliver saw this as an opportunity for Bud, who would soon be turning seventeen, to contribute to the family while also having a chance to see a different part of the country. As soon as he was eligible, Oliver took Bud to the local office of the Department of Labor and signed him up for a camp in New Mexico. Bud had no objections since he was eager to start a life of his own and he happily waved goodbye to his family the following month as he boarded the train for his assignment.

* * * *

As Oliver's other three sons got older, they seemed to come up with more and more ways to cause havoc – or have some fun as they saw it! Living in town was a new experience and they took advantage of all the opportunities this new life had to offer three young boys who were mostly unsupervised. There was a tailor living in the apartment just under the Nordmarks and he became a favorite target for the brothers' pranks. Suffering from bouts of intemperance, the man could often be found staggering down the sidewalk in the early evenings. When the boys saw him coming, they'd quickly fill up a pan with water, race to the window, and dump it onto his head. Then they'd slam the window down and run to the back of the house as the tailor filled the air with threats and profanity.

Raising cane with the German shoemakers who lived in a second downstairs apartment was easy since the cobblers were elderly and, try as they might, could never catch up with the young boys. On a regular basis, Jim and Benny would pound on their back door, then run around and pound on their front door until finally they would come out and begin chasing the youngsters down the sidewalk. Sometimes Benny would take particular delight in letting one of the shoemakers get almost close enough to grab him when suddenly Benny would drop to the ground. The man would go flying over him, spilling all over the sidewalk while Benny quickly changed direction and was out of sight before the shoemaker could gather his wits about him to resume the chase.

All of the neighbors complained to Oliver about his boys but Oliver usually just shrugged off their whining, preferring to think that his boys were just having fun and doing the sorts of things that all boys did.

Of course the brothers also entertained themselves with less threatening activities. Oliver found some used clamp-on roller skates at the Salvation Army and brought them home for his sons to use. With so many sidewalks in town, they would spend hours and hours cruising all over Stroudsburg on their first set of wheels. During winter months, when snow would cover the streets, all the kids in town enjoyed sledding on hilly 8th Street. Sometimes the boys would slam down their sleds behind slowly moving cars and hitch a ride on their bumpers for blocks and blocks until the drivers finally realized they were there, shouting for them to let go.

*   *   *   *

It was a happy life, but a poor life as well. Oliver was still working for the WPA but hours for each man on relief had been cut back. Benny would sometimes watch as his dad worked with other men digging up the road on Monroe Street to prepare it for paving. He resolved to find ways to earn some money himself, and began with soda bottles. The large soda bottles that he gathered up were marked with "5 cent deposit". That meant that the bottle could be returned to the store to be used again and the shopkeeper would pay you a nickel for it. Benny would scour the town looking behind the shops and in the alleys for discarded bottles. Once when he was behind Wycoff's Department Store, he noticed a small outdoor storage room. The door was opened and he crept up and peeked inside. It was full of empty bottles that had been returned to the store and which would later be sent back to the manufacturer to be used again. What an opportunity! Benny took four of the returned bottles from the back of the store, marched around the front of the store, and returned the bottles again for five cents each!

Next, Benny found that old newspapers could be taken to Sam Rubbin's Junkyard and, depending on the size of the load, Sam would pay five or ten cents.

"What other kinds of junk do you pay for?" Benny asked Sam Rubbin as he collected his first nickel for a stack of newspapers.

"Well, plenty of stuff," Sam replied to the young entrepreneur. "Scraps of metal might be something you can find to bring in for a bit of money."

"Thanks!" Benny replied, eager to start looking. "I'll find some and bring it down."

Benny spent all his spare time searching behind stores and garages in Stroudsburg picking up any discarded metal lying on the ground and taking it in his beat-up little wagon to the junkyard for the few coins that Sam Rubbin would pay him. He soon became very knowledgeable about the different types of metals – aluminum, brass, and copper – and value of each. Copper, he found, paid the most so he always had his eye out for that.

One night in late summer, the Stroud Movie Theatre across from the apartment burned to the ground. The family woke in the night to the sounds of the fire trucks racing to the sight in their futile attempt to douse the flames and save the building. The following morning, the totally destroyed theatre lay in ruin and everyone remarked at how terrible it was that the building had burned and how sad it would be not to have the theatre. Benny, however, saw a chance to make a little money. When the onlookers had left to go about their business, he wandered through the burnt out building where he quickly spied the electrical box. His eyes lit up as he saw all that copper! As fast as he could, he ripped out all of the precious metal and ran with it directly to the junkyard. He made some *real* money that day!

* * * *

Benny used his small wagon for all sorts of gathering. He would often bring back scraps of discarded wood for his dad to burn in the cook stove. Once, he even used it to bring home an old ice box that he had found and gave it to the two shoemakers who had said they were looking for one. Unfortunately, Benny had misunderstood them when they said "ice box" since their German accent was so strong. What they really were looking for was a "nice box". No matter, Benny thought, as he wheeled the ice box down to the junkyard where he traded it for a few pennies.

As Christmas 1938 drew near, Benny and Jim decided that they would have a Christmas Tree even though their father had said there was no money for Christmas that year. With rickety wagon in tow, they scoured the town in search of a tree that no one would miss. At the bottom of Monroe Street, they found what they were looking for. There by the side of the road was a raggedy little tree with only a few limbs that had been partially knocked over during the repaving project earlier that year. The boys both took a hold of the thin trunk and with a simple yank, pulled it from the ground. They laid it across the wagon and took turns holding it in place as they hauled it all the way back to 6th Street.

"We don't have anything to stand it up in," Benny quickly realized as he glanced around the apartment.

"Here," Jim said as he headed towards the old potbelly stove. "We can stick it here in the coal bucket."

They moved the bucket away from the stove to make sure their Christmas Tree would not catch fire and went about making popcorn balls to decorate it. When they were finished, they stepped back to admire their little tree.

"Well," Jim smiled. "We may not be gettin' any presents, but at least we got us a Christmas Tree."

*   *   *   *

Two weeks later, when Christmas morning arrived, Benny and Jim were astonished to wake in their living room bedroom to find a shiny new wagon under their little tree!

CHAPTER TWELVE

The World's Fair

In February of 1939, Oliver read a story in the newspaper about The World's Fair that would be opening on April 30th. It would be held in New York to celebrate the 150th anniversary of George Washington's first inauguration. Reading on, he found that the fair would have seven major areas including entertainment, food, amusements, and communications.

"Geez," Oliver thought to himself as he put down the newspaper. "Wouldn't the kids get a kick outta goin' to the World's Fair!"

Oliver quickly devised a plan to get his family to New York to see the fair, even if there wasn't any money to do much of anything once they got there. At least, he reasoned, they could see the unusual buildings that the article spoke of. There would be a two hundred foot round ball called the Perisphere and a seven hundred foot spike called the Trylon. The paper had an artist's rendition of the two structures and Oliver was amazed. He started saving every penny he could towards the adventure but did not utter a word about his plan to his children, just in case it did not come to pass.

As soon as school was out that spring, Oliver gave his children the surprise of their lives!

The 1939 World's Fair - Trylon & Perisphere

"The World's Fair?" they shouted in amazement when they heard the news. "We're going to the World's Fair!" They could not believe their good fortune. Did their father rob a bank? Did he steal money from Doc Andrews or the Chinese Laundry down the street? Was he going to be arrested? They just could not fathom how they could possibly have enough money to go to the World's Fair, but not one of them questioned their father for fear of finding out that it was untrue.

When the day finally came, the children all piled into Oliver's old car, full of excitement and anticipation at the adventure that lay before them. Oliver had altered the rumble seat on the back of the car, fashioning it into a small truck-like bed. Several of the children could ride there while the rest of the family could fit into the car. To give them extra room – and a bit of excitement – Oliver let the younger children take turns sitting on his lap and steering the old jalopy as it chugged along towards the big city.

Arrival at the Fair Grounds found all the children bouncing with excitement and full of energy as they looked in awe at the large, unusual buildings that had been erected on the site. There were buildings from other countries with all sorts of exhibits and attractions. The most popular ride, attracting as many as 28,000 people a day, was Futurama. This was a futuristic ride that transported fairgoers through what the creator imagined the United States would look like in the year 1960. Although the family could not afford to go on the ride, they enjoyed reading about it on the many signs outside the attraction.

The one exhibit that impressed the Nordmark children the most was free of charge and presented by RCA. It was the debut of television and featured a televised speech by President Roosevelt. The tiny screen was part of a large radio that would transmit the sound. Everyone gathered around to view the fascinating new invention!

As they prepared to leave the fair at the end of the day, a stranger approached the rag-tag group and silently handed Oliver two passes for the rollercoaster. After realizing what they were, Oliver looked up to thank the man, but he was already gone.

"Well, I guess we're going to go on a ride after all," Oliver announced as he showed the tickets to his children. "There's two passes for the Bobsled Rollercoaster so Oliver, why don't you take Jim."

The boys couldn't believe their good fortune. The entire family took off running towards the rollercoaster, excited to see the boys ride the lightning-fast wooden monster.

"You get in the front, Jim," Oliver Jr. directed. "I'll sit here behind you. It's sort of like riding a sled."

The boys climbed aboard with broad smiles as they waved to the rest of the family. The train of bobsleds began inching forward, then slowly picked up speed. As they began to climb the first hill, the clanking chains and creaking wood sounds caused Jim to cry out in fright. In a panic, he stood up in the bobsled, shouting and waving his hands to get out.

"Jim!" Oliver Jr. shouted to his brother. "Sit down, Jim!" he commanded as he pulled hard on his brother's shirt.

Jim, who was confused and frightened, spent the entire two minute ride screaming and trying to stand up to get off the rollercoaster. Oliver Jr. meanwhile spent the ride trying to keep his brother from falling to a certain death out of the bobsled. By the time the ride came to a stop, both boys were exhausted and more than ready to get off the rollercoaster.

"I hate that!" Jim screamed as he climbed out of the bobsled. "I'm never going on a rollercoaster again as long as I live!"

"And I'm never going on one again with YOU!" Oliver Jr. shouted back to his brother. "You're crazy, Jim! Trying to get out of a moving rollercoaster. You're lucky I didn't just let you jump!"

As the family ran up to greet the boys, everyone was shouting with excitement as they shared their stories of the ride.

"Okay, okay now," Oliver quieted his children. "Let's head to the car now. It's a long ride home."

May & Edgar's Wedding

CHAPTER THIRTEEN

May and Edgar

Having returned from The World's Fair, May decided it was time to put her plans for her future in play. She had recently graduated from high school and hoped to soon be working as a bookkeeper for Wycoff's Department Store. Whenever possible, she would sneak off to spend time with Edgar, who already had a job at Wycoff's.

Although a little nervous on her first job interview, May sailed through the questions with relative ease and had no problems with the math and bookkeeping tests that were required. She was offered the position before she left and was excited to begin work, looking forward to having a little money of her own.

Oliver, however, had other plans. With May working, he expected her to contribute to the household expenses and she was heartbroken when he told her that she would need to give him half of her twelve dollar weekly salary.

"Half?" May asked, hardly believing her ears. "Six dollars a week?"

"It will help to put food on the table," he explained. "And help with the rent and coal bills. Winter will be here before you know it."

May quickly relented and dutifully handed over half of her paycheck at the end of each week. Meanwhile, she and Edgar were making plans.

"We have to save up everything we make," Edgar explained his thoughts to May. "That way we'll have enough to get a place of our own by September – October at the latest. Then we can get married."

The couple had already pledged their love for one another and had often spoken of the day when they could get married. Now May could see that it was within her grasp. She kept her plans a secret, feeling certain that she knew how her father would react.

"You can't get married!" Oliver protested when May finally shared the news of her approaching nuptials. "You're too young, May. And besides, you barely know this Edgar Hall."

"I'm not too young, I'm nineteen," May protested. "And Edgar and I have been dating since we were in high school so we know each other just fine!"

"Since high school? What do you mean since high school?" Oliver asked. May had lived with the Kemmerers for most of her high school years and Oliver knew that Edgar and his brother Kenney had lived there too.

"Well," May knew she had shared a bit too much. "Yes, we started dating in high school, but we kept it quiet at first." She figured she might as well spill the beans now. She had nothing to lose, and she was past the age of consent.

"I don't approve of your marryin' him," Oliver objected. "But I know I got no say in it, so go on and do what you're gonna do."

He left the room, leaving May with her thoughts. She shouldn't have told him about dating Edgar in high school since they were living under the same roof at the Kemmerers, but what was done was done and there was no taking it back now. She grabbed her purse and headed out to share this latest update with Edgar.

$$* \quad * \quad * \quad *$$

May Elizabeth Nordmark and Edgar Hall, Jr. were united in marriage on October 1, 1939. May had saved enough money to buy a beautiful white gown with ruffled square neckline and gathered bodice. Her long, lace-edged veil draped gracefully over each shoulder and she carried a large bouquet of white roses. Ruth and Marv Williams, who were May and Edgar's best friends, stood as witnesses for the couple.

The newlyweds settled quietly in a small apartment on Main Street in Stroudsburg. May was thrilled to be able to keep all her pay for the first time in her life, but she didn't forget the family she left behind. When Wycoff's had a sale on boy's clothing, she purchased new knickers, knee socks, dress shirts, and shoes for Jim and Benny. Every Sunday, she would go and get her youngest brothers from 6th Street, and bring them to her apartment to change into their Sunday clothes. Together with her new husband, the four of them would attend church services just as she had during her years at the Kemmerers' home. After church, they would return to the Main Street apartment where the boys would change out of their good clothes, leaving them with May until the following week. Having been the only "mother" that Jim and Benny could remember, she found it difficult to shake her role in their lives and intended to continue taking them to church and helping them in any other way she could, for as long as they needed her.

CHAPTER FOURTEEN

The Sealed Envelope

With Bud in the CCC and May married and living on Main Street, only Margaret, Oliver Jr., Jim and Benny remained at home in the 6th Street apartment. Fall quickly turned into winter and Oliver felt a growing sense of dread and hopelessness. He had done the best he could for his family but with the loss of his wife Estella so many years ago, it had been difficult, to say the least. With the added burden of the Great Depression, a lack of steady work, very little pay from the WPA and no hope in sight, Oliver felt beaten down. He often lay awake at night wondering just where things would lead and questioning what he could have done differently over the years. In late November of 1939, something in him broke, causing him to do the unthinkable.

As his children left for school that morning, Oliver handed Oliver Jr. a sealed envelope.

"Slip this inside your pocket," Oliver instructed. "Don't open it till you get back home this afternoon."

"Okay, Dad," Oliver Jr. smiled as he stashed the envelope into the inside pocket of his coat and grabbed his lunch pail.

Oliver bent down and kissed the head of his youngest son Benny.

"Be a good boy," he told the ten-year-old.

Benny grabbed his lunch pail too and took off with Jim, briefly thinking that it was a bit strange that his dad had kissed him on the head – he had never done that before.

The children trotted off to school and upon returning that afternoon to the 6th Street apartment, found no one home and wondered where their father was.

"He's probably out somewhere," Oliver Jr. reasoned as he flopped on one of the sofas. "He'll be back sooner or later."

It was Jim who remembered the envelope. "Open the envelope like Dad said and read it," he told Oliver Jr.

"Oh yeah," said Oliver Jr. as he reached inside his pocket and tore open the envelope thoughtlessly.

Oliver Jr. skimmed through the note quickly than sat back down and read it out loud to his brothers and sister.

"Take this to Miss Martin at the Children's Aid Society office as soon as you read it," Oliver Jr. began as he read the first line of the note. "Dear Miss Martin, Please help my children. I cannot see a future for them living like this. I have tried. I am sorry. Oliver Nordmark."

Oliver Jr. folded up the note and put it back in the envelope. There was just a moment of quiet before Benny and Jim reacted. Coming and going in and out of their father's life was a pattern that had repeated itself before.

"Well come on," Jim nudged his older brother. "Let's go and see Miss Martin."

"Yeah," smiled Benny. "Maybe we'll get to go to a farm again!"

"And maybe they'll have horses and we'll get a pony of our own," Jim imagined.

"And we can play Cowboys and Indians, Jim!" Benny said as he became more and more excited. "I can be the Lone Ranger and you can be Tonto!"

"I'm older," Jim corrected. "So I'm gonna be the Lone Ranger and you can be my sidekick Tonto."

Margaret and Oliver Jr. remained quiet, having a deeper appreciation at the age of fourteen and fifteen respectively, of just what this meant. They were leaving their father again, headed for their third foster home, and who knew if they'd ever be back together again.

"Okay," Oliver replied. "Let's go and see what Miss Martin's got in store for us."

*　*　*　*

"Oh dear," Miss Martin sighed as she read the note. "Your dad must be really feeling down and out. But don't you worry, we'll figure something out."

The children sat down in the hard chairs that

lined the walls of the Children's Aid Society office. Miss Martin quickly picked up the phone and began to make several calls. Eventually she rose from her desk and went over to speak to the children.

"Margaret," she began with the only girl in the group. "I've spoken with the Kemmerers, and they would be very happy to have you come back and stay with them. Now isn't that wonderful?"

"That's fine," Margaret replied, resigned to her placement. At least she knew what to expect at the Kemmerers. They were a good Christian couple and they treated her fairly.

"Now you boys," Miss Martin began slowly, trying to make sure she presented the solution in a way that would not upset them. "There doesn't seem to be anyone who can take all three of you together, at least not right now." She tried to gauge their reactions but found no clues on their young faces. "Jim, you and Oliver Jr. will be going to the Warners' farm out in Gilbert. Benny, you'll be going to Shawnee Valley to a farm owned by Wendell and Alice Wicks."

"I wanna go with my brothers," a frightened Benny protested.

"Now don't you worry," Miss Martin consoled him. "Mr. and Mrs. Wicks are very nice people and I'm sure there will be lots of chances to visit with your brothers."

Benny was not convinced, but he gave up his protest and began worrying about what it would be like without any of his brothers with him.

* * * *

A short time later, Miss Martin gathered her things and instructed Benny to come with her.

"Mrs. Kemmerer is on her way over to pick you up, Margaret," Miss Martin smiled at the young girl. "And one of the other aid workers will be along shortly to take you boys out to Gilbert. I'm going to head over to Shawnee with Benny."

The children said their good-byes and Benny tagged along behind Miss Martin, climbing into the back seat of her car which was parked just out front.

"We're going to stop at J. C. Penney to get you some new clothes before we head over to the Wicks' farm," Miss Martin said as she smiled in the rearview mirror at the young boy.

Benny was surprised and delighted as he followed Miss Martin through the aisles of the large department store. She bought him three pairs of new trousers, new shoes, and a brand new winter coat.

"Wow, I've really hit pay dirt this time around," he thought to himself.

They loaded everything into the car and headed for Shawnee Valley. The Wicks' farm was situated on the side of a hill and Benny climbed dutifully up the front steps of the farmhouse behind Miss Martin. They were greeted by a smiling woman in an apron with gently curled red hair and freckles on her face.

"Well, who have we here?" she smiled as she welcomed Benny into the front room.

"This is Benny Nordmark," Miss Martin said by way of introduction. "We've purchased some new things which ought to be enough to get him through the winter." Miss Martin handed the packages over to the farmer's wife.

"Well, I'm very glad to meet you, Benny. I'm Alice Wicks, and my husband Wendell and I are very happy to have you staying with us," the red haired lady said with a smile as she reached out to shake Benny's hand.

Benny quietly shook Alice Wicks' hand then looked up as Miss Martin spoke.

"Well, I'll be getting back to town now. Just let me know if you need anything," Miss Martin said to them as she turned to go.

* * * *

Alice Wicks took Benny up the wooden stairs of the large farmhouse and showed him into his new bedroom. Benny looked around in amazement. The large room had beautiful wide plank floors varnished to a gleaming shine. There were two long windows, a large double bed with soft, handmade quilts and fluffy pillows, and a tall wooden chest of drawers.

"Now I'll just give you time to get settled in

and put your clothes and other things away, Benny," Alice smiled. "After you're finished, come on downstairs because it will be time for dinner."

"Is this whole room just for me?" Benny quietly asked.

"Well, yes," Alice replied. "If there's anything more you need, you be sure to tell me, okay?"

"Oh, this is plenty," Benny answered as he gently touched the soft bedding.

"See you downstairs," Alice said as she left the room to go and finish preparing the evening meal.

Benny walked slowly around the room as he lightly touched all the fine things that were now part of his space. He sat carefully on the double bed, as so many thoughts raced through his mind. He was thinking about his brothers and hoping that they were just as lucky. He wondered about his father and how he would know where to find him when he was ready to take him back again. Slowly he went about the task of emptying the packages of new clothing and putting things into the drawers. When everything was neatly put away, and there was nothing else for him to do, Benny sat again on the edge of the bed, not wanting to go downstairs. He had a desperate feeling of being all alone with two strange adults and didn't understand why these people couldn't take his brothers too so that they could all stay together.

Benny wasn't sure how much time had slipped by, but eventually there was a soft knock on the bedroom door.

"May I come in?" Alice Wicks asked as she poked her head in the door.

"Yes," Benny replied with his head lowered.

"Dinner's all ready and waiting on the table," she coaxed the young boy.

"I'm not hungry," Benny answered, arms folded across his chest.

"Oh sure you are," Alice smiled as she took Benny by the hand. "I'm sure you're very hungry after such a long day."

Benny slid off the bed and followed Alice Wicks out of his new bedroom and down the stairs to the farmhouse dining room. Taking his place at the table, he was amazed at all the food before him. There was a simmering beef stew, a fresh garden salad, warm rolls and butter, and even a dish of homemade applesauce. His glass was filled to the brim with sweet tea and as Benny reached to help himself, Alice Wicks lightly touched his hand in correction as she began a blessing of thanks to the Lord for the bounty of food before them as well as for the newest addition to their family.

* * * *

"I'd say its time to turn in now," Wendell Wicks suggested to young Benny later that evening. "We'll get you set up tomorrow at your new school. Mrs. Wicks will take you over and get you all settled in, then you can ride the school bus back home at the end of the day."

"Okay, I'll be ready first thing in the morning," Benny quietly replied as he headed up the steps and into his new bedroom.

Once upstairs, Benny quickly changed into his night clothes and climbed into his new bed. He sank into the thick soft mattress and pulled the sheets and quilts up to his face, taking a deep breath to smell the freshly laundered bedding. His thoughts quickly drifted to his brothers and sister. The foster homes that they had been in together had never been like the Wicks' home. The people had never been as nice, and the food had never been so plentiful. Benny wondered where his brothers were and how they were making out. He wished so much that they were here with him now and he wondered how long it would be before he could have a visit with them. As his thoughts drifted off, there was a light tapping at the door.

"May I come in?" asked Alice Wicks softly.

Benny nodded in her direction.

"Well, I see you've gotten yourself all set for the night," Alice began as she reached for the spare blanket and tucked it up under Benny's chin. "It gets a little chilly in the night, so you'll probably be happy to have an extra blanket."

Then something happened that took Benny by complete surprise. Alice Wicks bent down and kissed the ten-year-old on the forehead.

"Goodnight Benny," Alice smiled. "I hope you

Back: Wendell Wicks, Benny, Alice Wicks
Front: Zandee, Sue and Thad Wicks

will be happy here with us."

"Goodnight," was all that a near speechless Benny could say in reply. It was the first time anyone had ever tucked him into bed and kissed him goodnight. It felt good, but it also felt a little strange.

As she turned and headed out the bedroom door, Alice Wicks had one more thing to say. "Oh, and I'll have a lunch packed for you to take to school tomorrow. I've baked some chocolate cupcakes, so I'll put one in for a treat."

Benny smiled a wide grin as Alice closed the door softly behind her.

"I'm going to have *cupcakes*!" he thought to himself with glee. As he rolled over and began to drift off to sleep, he decided that he must be the luckiest boy on Earth and he looked forward with excitement to see what other treats this new life might bring! "It's like I'm trading peanut butter for cupcakes after all," Benny thought to himself. "And I'm thinkin' maybe that's only the beginning!"

Margaret & May

EPILOGUE

May & Margaret

May Elizabeth Nordmark remained in Stroudsburg with her new husband Edgar Hall. Her first child, Laura May, was born in 1943. As the first of Oliver's grandchildren, she was happily spoiled by all her uncles. Two sons followed, Edgar Oliver and Bruce Theodore. In 1958 the family relocated to Santa Maria, CA. Edgar passed away in 1984 at the age of 64 and May died in 1985 at the age of 65. May's heart had been damaged by rheumatic fever as a child and she died of heart failure. She and Edgar have six grandchildren and two step-grandchildren. Laura May now makes her home in Georgia, Ted is in Maryland, and Ed remains in California.

Margaret Loraine Nordmark remained in the Stroudsburg area where she married James Treible. They had two daughters, Patty and Holly. The marriage eventually ended in divorce and Margaret later married John Baabe. During her early retirement years, she spent winters in Florida, returning to Stroudsburg for the warmer months. She is now eighty-three and lives full-time in Stroudsburg with her husband John.

Bud & Oliver, Jr.

Francis (Bud) & Oliver Jr.

Francis Henry Nordmark returned from the Civilian Conservation Corp and soon married Doris Arnold. They had two children, Michael and Sandy, before the marriage ended in divorce. Bud then married Rose Oliveri and had two more children, Robert and Bonnie. With his third wife Ann, Bud had 2 sons, Donald and Alan. Having also been stricken as a child with rheumatic fever, Bud required heart surgery in 1962. On October 2nd, he died on the operating table at the age of 40. At last record, all of Bud's children live in Pennsylvania.

Oliver Edward Nordmark stayed a few weeks at the Warner farm before he asked Miss Martin if he could return to the Balliets. At eighteen, he enlisted in the Navy where he worked on submarines. After the Navy, Oliver worked first for a dry cleaning company earning $52.00 a month, and then for the U.S. Post Office. He married Jean Dickisson and together they had three sons; Albert, Ralph and Ted. Oliver and Jean raised their family in the Stroudsburg area, where two of his sons still reside. Oliver's wife Jean passed away in 1993. He is now eighty-four and living in Stroudsburg where he enjoys reading and spending time with his family.

Jim

Benny

Jim & Benny

James Bruce Nordmark remained on the Warner farm in Gilbert for several years. Floyd Warner was a sharecropper and a drinker and Jim was treated poorly. On one occasion, Jim took a dead snake and playfully shook it in front of the Warners' granddaughters. They ran in the house screaming and within seconds, Mrs. Warner came out chasing Jim with a board in her hand. She caught up to him in the wagon shed and gave him a severe beating. Eventually Oliver found out about the way Jim was being treated and he came to the farm to confront Floyd Warner. Jim was removed from their care and placed with his sister at the Kemmerers. He was later replaced to the home of Ferman Singer, a farmer who lived in the neighboring town of McMichael. He was treated much better at the Singers' and on Saturday nights enjoyed walking into town to play "horse and pepper" in a little store owned by Phil Kishpaugh. This would be Jim's last foster care placement. Next, he worked for room and board at the Kresge farm and at the age of sixteen, his father got him a job at the Sun Shipyards in Sharon Hill, PA. Jim soon decided that he wanted to join the service but he was too young. He bought an ink eradicator, changed the date on his birth certificate, and ran off to try and sign-up. The Army, Navy, and

Marines refused to take him, but Jim persisted. When he approached the Coast Guard recruiter, he was signed up on the spot – they didn't even ask to see his birth certificate! Oliver argued that his son was too young, but Jim convinced him that the Coast Guard only patrolled around the U.S. and that he would be perfectly safe. Jim left for boot camp and before he was seventeen, he was on a destroyer headed to the Mediterranean Sea. He didn't know that during wartime, the Coast Guard was under the direction of the Navy. Upon his return, Jim drifted from job to job, staying with friends. He joined a traveling carnival where he performed on a motorcycle in the motor drone, and hitchhiked to Kansas with his friend "Moon". When they ran out of money, his sister May wired him fifty dollars to come home. Eventually, Jim met and married Muriel Jones. They settled in Saylorsburg where Jim worked at the Post Office. They have four children; Steve, Debbie, Jimmy and Joann who all still live in the Stroudsburg area. Jim, who is now eighty-two, and Muriel live in Palmerton, PA.

Benjamin Elvin Nordmark remained at the Wicks' farm until he was eighteen and joined the Navy. Wendell and Alice, both Cornell University alumni, treated Benny as a member of the family. Wendell taught Benny how to budget money, giving him an allowance of thirty cents per week and a ledger book to keep track of his "finances".

Benny learned all the chores of farming including milking 16 cows and feeding 2000 hens. By age eleven he was spending eight hours a day preparing, plowing, and fertilizing the fields. He did well in school under Alice Wicks' watchful eye, graduating at the top of his class in 8th grade where he received the honor of valedictorian. The Wicks' later had three children; Sue, Zandee and Thad. Wendell died in 1975 and Alice lived to be 90, passing away in 2006. Together they owned and operated the Quiet Valley Living Farm Museum near Stroudsburg. Living with the Wicks' from the age of ten, Benny was fortunate to have the love and care of true parents in his final foster care placement. Wendell and Alice Wicks gave witness to the value of hard work, the commitment needed for a loving and successful marriage, as well as the importance of giving back to one's community. They knew just how to turn 'peanut butter into cupcakes' for one small boy.

In 1952, Ben married Sara Anne Hall of West Chester, PA. They settled in Kennett Square, PA where they raised five children; Ben Jr., Dawn, Donna, Brian, and Allison. Retiring in 1984 after twenty-seven years with IBM, Ben is now seventy-nine and lives with his wife in West Grove, PA where they can be close to four of their five children and many of their thirteen grandchildren.

Oliver Nordmark

Oliver

After several years, a settlement of $6,000 was reached with the Indian Queen Hotel over the death of Estella Nordmark. The money was held by the Children's Aid Society for the care of Estella's children.

Oliver lived to be ninety-five years old. Having been abandoned by his own parents at the age of six, Oliver and his younger brother were placed in the Children's Village Orphanage on Long Island, NY. One year later, they were chosen to ride one of America's Orphan Trains to Kansas in search of a home. His early life is the subject of the author's first two books, *Fly Little Bird, Fly!* and *Beyond The Orphan Train.*

Having never had parents of his own as a child, Oliver was ill-equipped to raise six children. The Great Depression placed an added burden on him and, try as he might, he was not able to provide a stable home for his family. He was a gentle, kind man, and his sons remember that he always stood up for them, and protected them as best he knew how. He rarely disciplined them, but rather looked upon their behavior as no more than the antics of young boys looking for ways to have some fun. Perhaps he caught glimpses of himself in his own sons and was trying to give them the playful childhood he had missed.

Present Day 6th Street Apartment

Present Day House on Brushy Mountain

Present Day Bungalow on Route 209

Present Day Cottage at Cherry Valley

DISCUSSION QUESTIONS

1. Oliver blamed himself for Estella's death, saying that he never should have let her take that job. Was his self-blame justified?

2. Why do you think that some of the foster homes proved to be unloving and harsh environments for the children?

3. What hardships did the boys have when compared to your life? What freedoms did they have?

4. Why did Oliver Sr. allow his boys to run wild and unsupervised?

5. Discuss the "adventures and pranks" of the Nordmark brothers. Do you think it was all just "fun" or was their behavior a problem?

6. Is stealing coal justified if your family has no heat?

7. Why do you think Oliver chose to turn his four younger children over to the Children's Aid Society a second time? Why did he choose to tell them in a letter?

8. Why did the author choose to end the book with Benny's first day at the Wicks?

ABOUT THE AUTHOR

 Donna Nordmark Aviles, the grand-daughter of Oliver and Estella Nordmark, lives with her family in Hockessin, Delaware. Her first two books, *Fly Little Bird, Fly!* and *Beyond The Orphan Train* are the true story of Oliver's childhood as an orphan train rider at the turn of the century. Both books have been named the winner of the 2009 BEST BOOKS Award, sponsored by USA Book News, in the Audiobook – Non Fiction category. *Peanut Butter For Cupcakes* was named a finalist in the Next Generation Indie Book Awards for 2009 as well as a finalist in the 2009 BEST BOOKS Award contest.

Aviles enjoys visiting schools and community organizations to speak about the Orphan Train Movement and The Great Depression. To learn more, visit her on the web at www.orphantrainbook.com.

"It's very American, their journey to find their places in the world. I'm attracted to true stories and these have a lot of heart, drama, humor and adventure. She's a young writer, new to the craft, and she's able to accomplish that. It's very difficult."

-William Rotko, Screenwriter
Los Angeles, CA

CPSIA information can be obtained at www.ICGtesting.com
Printed in the USA
BVOW01s1729190315

392258BV00001B/2/P